100

THINGS TO DO IN
ANNAPOLIS
AND THE EASTERN SHORE
BEFORE YOU
DIE

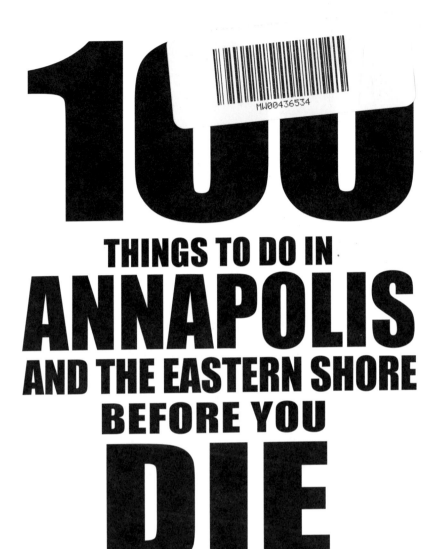

Photo courtesy of Susan Moynihan

100

THINGS TO DO IN
ANNAPOLIS
AND THE EASTERN SHORE
BEFORE YOU
DIE

SUSAN MOYNIHAN

REEDY PRESS

Library of Congress Control Number: 2019936701

ISBN: 9781681062136

Design by Jill Halpin

Printed in the United States of America
19 20 21 22 23   5 4 3 2 1

Please note that websites, phone numbers, addresses, and company names are subject
to change or cancellation. We did our best to relay the most accurate information
available, but due to circumstances beyond our control, please do not hold us liable for
misinformation. When exploring new destinations, please do your homework before
you go.

DEDICATION

To Dad, for bringing me home.

CONTENTS

• •

Music and Entertainment

• •

• •

• •

xi

PREFACE

Welcome to my 100-point love letter to my home: Annapolis and Maryland's Eastern Shore. Annapolis is the state capital, and one of the prettiest towns in the United States, home to thriving contemporary culture grown out of centuries-old roots. The Eastern Shore is the right-hand flank of the Chesapeake Bay, with marshes, farmland, and waterways extending to the Atlantic Ocean; the Maryland part of the greater Delmarva peninsula. Annapolis and the Eastern Shore both center around the Chesapeake Bay; the largest estuary in the United States, it is the lifeblood of the region. To experience one and not the other means you're missing out; that's why they're here, together, as one book.

We moved to Annapolis when I was thirteen, and though I've moved away and back, it has always been home. My father was a Naval officer who retired early, choosing to land in the home town of the U.S. Naval Academy. He traveled the world long before I did, but after finding Annapolis, his wanderlust faded. "I live in the best place in the world," he'd say. "Why would I go anywhere else?"

As a resident Annapolitan, I totally understand. April marks the beginning of boating season, and who could miss that? Come fall, our vibrant red maple trees rival anything in New England, especially when they're reflected in calm Bay waters. Winter brings the chance to curl up in front of the same centuries-old fireplaces that warmed our rebellious forefathers. Summer is all about celebration, exploration, and mighty fine eating due to our beloved crustaceans.

What you will find inside: Boats, water and plentiful ways to enjoy them, because that's how we roll by the Chesapeake Bay. There's history, because we have more than 400 years of it. There's food, sourced from these waters and grown on this land. (Yes, you'll find crabs. Multiple times.) And there are festivals. Because Marylanders love an excuse for a party, the quirkier the better. (That means you, Eastport.)

I kept my focus on ideas that reflect, embody or are created by the people who live here. These 100 experiences couldn't exist any other place in the world. Most of all, these picks are personal. These are the things I do on my own, that I share with visiting friends and family, and that I cite when people ask me why I love where I live.

To my Bay neighbors, I know I may be missing something you love. The truth is (and I'm sure you agree), 100 experiences are not nearly enough to touch on all of the aspects that make our region so special. Visitors, you're about to find that out first-hand.

Whatever your motivation is for picking up this book, I hope it gives you reasons to get out and explore this unique part of the world—100 of them, actually.

—Susan Moynihan

• •

ACKNOWLEDGMENTS

A special thanks to everyone who shared their favorites, gave me feedback and helped me explore.

Ann Moynihan	Barbara Moynihan	Joy Moynihan
Pat Moynihan	Jeff Nicklason	Lynne Forstman
Susan Seifried	Megan Padilla	Liz Langley
Elvia Thompson	Jinny Amundson	Aida Cipriani
Catherine Eunice	Daphne Ferrier	Charlotte Faraci
Harley Hope	Mary Calhoun	Marshall Mentz
Old Fox Book Club	Diane Turner	Jennifer Kaye
Mike Carter	Tracy Johns	Nick Sottile
Lisa Challenger	Lisa Fontaine	Jordan Lloyd

Planning a trip? These are my go-to local resources to find out what's happening.

AnnapolisDiscovered.com
UpStArt Annapolis
Eye on Annapolis
Secrets of the Eastern Shore
Chesapeake Bay Monthly
What's Up Annapolis and What's Up Eastern Shore
Visit Annapolis
Visit Maryland

• •

Photo courtesy of Jeff Nicklason

FOOD AND DRINK

CHOMP A CRAB CAKE
CHESAPEAKE-STYLE

If there is one dish that defines this region, it's the crab cake, found on menus from dive bars to five-star restaurants. By various accounts, the humble dish traces its origins either to the original Native Americans here or the English settlers who adapted their homeland minced-meat patties to incorporate the Bay's abundant crustaceans.

We Marylanders are deeply picky about our cakes; I won't eat them outside of Maryland because they never measure up. And we all have our favorite recipe, often passed down through the family. But the common denominator is crab meat (lump only, please), a moistening agent (egg or mayo), and a hint of binding agent or seasoning; Maryland tradition is to use as little filler as possible, just enough to hold the meat together. Get a taste of what I mean at one of these three restaurants, known for having the best crabcakes around.

BOATYARD BAR & GRILL

The oversized cakes at this beloved sailors' bar bear the slogan "all killer, no filler" and are served broiled to perfection. Jimmy Buffet and I are fans.

400 Fourth St.
410-216-6206
boatyardbarandgrill.com

WATERMAN'S CRAB HOUSE

Enjoy sunset-facing views as you eat up award-winning cakes in the boating enclave of Rock Hall.

21055 W. Sharp St., Rock Hall
410-639-2261
watermanscrabhouse.com

EDGEWATER RESTAURANT

This unpretentious, old-school eatery hasn't changed much since opening in 1948, and that's the appeal— along with meaty lump crab cakes that draw diehard fans from all over Delmarva.

148 Mayo Rd., Edgewater
410-956-3202

GET PICKING
AT A MARYLAND CRAB HOUSE

The best crabs in the world come from the Chesapeake Bay, and the best place to eat them is at an authentic Maryland crab house. How do you know you're in the right place? The vibe is always casual, with indoor/outdoor seating, long family-style tables covered in butcher paper, and a dock outside for diners who come by boat. The crabs are steamed rather than boiled, as you find farther south. (It keeps the meat moister.)

Crustaceans are served by the dozen, piled on a tray and dumped in the center of the table for easy access. You'll get melted butter and Old Bay for dipping; sides of fresh corn, coleslaw, and rolls; and local beer (preferably Natty Boh) to wash it down. Dining is a slow process, especially for newbies as they maneuver the best way to get the meat from the crab's various crevices. But the slow pace is part of the joy, with the focus as much on together time as it is on eating.

JIMMY CANTLER'S RIVERSIDE INN

Don't let the hours-long lines and busloads of tourists dissuade you. Wood-paneled Cantler's is the real deal, started in 1974 by a fifth-generation waterman.

458 Forest Beach Rd.
410-757-1311
cantlers.com

MIKE'S CRAB HOUSE

This circa-1958 spot on the South River is where locals go when they want to avoid the crowds at Cantler's; plentiful docking space is a bonus.

3030 Riva Rd., Edgewater
410-956-2784
mikescrabhouse.com

FISHERMAN'S CRAB DECK

Sitting on the waterfront deck, listening to live music, and feasting on fresh crabs is about as summer as you can get (and it's not open in the winter).

3032 Kent Narrows Way North, Grasonville
410-827-6666
crabdeck.com

TALK CRAB
LIKE AN ANNAPOLITAN

Want to talk crabs like a local? Memorize these terms.

Soft shells: Crabs molt approximately twenty times in their lives, going twelve hours without a hard shell. They're a delicacy, typically served sauteed or lightly battered and fried.

Jumbo lump: The best part of the crab, these firm chunks of cartilage-free meat come from the muscles of the swimming fins, and are perfect for dipping in drawn butter.

Backfin: Shredded-texture meat comes from the body of the crab; this is what's used in most soup and imperial recipes.

Jimmys: Male crabs are typically larger and therefore easier to eat, which means they're also most prized. A #1 or Colossal crab is a Jimmy that's six inches or longer, tip to tip.

Sooks: Female crabs are smaller and less expensive, but are said to have sweeter meat.

Mustard: The fat of the crab, officially called *tomalley*, is greenish in color and an acquired taste I haven't acquired.

Roe: The bright-orange eggs found in female crabs are considered a delicacy and often used as a seasoning.

LAY INTO A CAKE
AT A SMITH ISLAND BAKERY

The unique layered cake that is Maryland's official state dessert has its roots on isolated Smith Island. One legend has it that generations ago, island women would compete to create cakes for community cake walks, and the ones with the thinnest, most stackable layers would earn the most money. I've also heard that women would bake one layer for each hour their waterman husbands were out at sea; the more layers you had, the more hard-working your man. Either way, the result is this torte-style cake, traditionally eight to ten layers of yellow cake iced with a chocolate fudge frosting. In the 1800s, when the watermen would head out for the autumn oyster harvest, Smith Island wives would send cakes along to remind them of home. Today, they're a tradition all over Maryland, and you'll find them in flavors such as lemon and red velvet as well as the classic chocolate-and-vanilla combo. Two companies make them at or near the source. In 2009, Smith Island Baking Co. opened an on-island bakery, sending cakes by boat to the mainland for delivery across the country. As demand outpaced the limitations of shipping cakes via ferry, they relocated to mainland Crisfield for easier distribution. In 2017, Smith Island Bakery opened on island in Ewell, selling fresh cakes to visitors who prefer their confections made on the motherland.

45 W. Chesapeake Ave., Crisfield, 410-425-CAKE, smithislandcake.com

20926 Caleb Jones Rd., Suite B, Ewell, 410-425-2018
facebook.com/smithislandbakery

SIP SOME VINO
AT VIN 909

Vin 909 Winecafe is one of my favorite spots in Annapolis—and the same goes for my fellow Annapolitans, evidenced by the sometimes-hour-long wait for a table in this cheery wooden cottage in Eastport. But it's worth it when you're finally seated on the covered outdoor patio and dig into their toothsome brick-oven pizzas and seasonal small plates like fresh-pulled mozzarella, seared gnocchi, or savory clams, all made with locally sourced organic produce in the open-view kitchen. The wide-ranging wine list spans sixty-plus varietals (all available by glass or bottle), sourced from around the world and reasonably priced from six to twelve dollars per glass. It's the kind of place where you just want to linger—which, come to think of it, is probably why there's such a long wait.

909 Bay Ridge Ave.
410-990-1846
vin909.com

PLEDGE TO CHOW DOWN
AT CHICK & RUTH'S DELLY

Chick and Ruth Levitt changed the face of Main Street when they opened Chick & Ruth's Delly in 1965, growing it from a small sandwich shop to a full-service diner and Annapolis institution. Despite new ownership in 2017, not much has changed, from the open grill and vintage chrome counter, bright yellow-and-orange color scheme and walls crammed with signed celebrity promo shots to the tiny laminate tables, separated by low cubicle walls for a hint of privacy. The ten-page menu covers diner classics from omelets to burgers. Or you can order from the wall, plastered with bright, circular signs listing sandwiches named after area politicians. I'm partial to the "Senator John Astle" (roast beef topped with french fries and gravy), but the cheesesteaks win raves, as do the crab cakes. Come hungry because portions are huge. Their six-pound milkshake was featured on *Man v. Food*, and that's just one of four daily Colossal Challenges.

165 Main St., 410-269-6737
chickandruths.com

TIP
In a tradition that's lasted thirty years (and counting), the staff leads patrons in the daily Pledge of Allegiance, held promptly at 8:30 a.m. weekdays, 9:30 a.m. weekends.

EAT JUNK FOOD
ON THE BOARDWALK

The Ocean City boardwalk opened in 1900 and has been ruining diets ever since. In a few short blocks, you can indulge in the same treats that your grandparents savored when they were kids. The original Dolle's Candyland has been serving up tasty saltwater taffy since 1910, along with fudge, caramel apples, and candied nuts. Across the boardwalk, Thrasher's French Fries opened in 1929 with the goal of selling the perfect french fry; the same principle is in effect today, garnering ever-present lines down the block for their Idaho potatoes fried in peanut oil and served with apple-cider vinegar and salt. Three blocks down, at circa-1937 Fisher's Popcorn, choose from copper kettle–popped corn flavored with butter, caramel, white cheddar, or even Old Bay. Want some culture with your snacks? Join OC Foodie Tour on a three-hour walking tour that pairs flavors with history.

Dolle's Candyland, 500 S. Boardwalk
800-337-6001, dolles.com

Thrasher's French Fries, 410 S. Atlantic Ave.
410-289-7232, thrashersfries.com

Fisher's Popcorn, 200 S. Boardwalk
888-395-0335, fisherspopcorn.com

OC Foodie Tour, 3303 Coastal Hwy.
443-497-0458, ocfoodietour.com

● ●

TIP

More vintage fun can be had at Trimper's Rides, home to a 1912 carousel and 1920s kiddie Ferris wheel. Or head to Marty's Playland to get your fix of vintage pinball and arcade games, including my favorite, a Zoltar fortune-telling machine from the 1940s.

DEVELOP A CRUSH
AT HARBORSIDE BAR & GRILL

Maryland's unofficial cocktail, the Orange Crush, is the perfect accompaniment to sitting by the water on a hot summer day. The drink was invented in 1995 at Harborside Bar & Grill, located bayside at Sunset Marina in West Ocean City, but you'll find them all over the region, in flavors like grapefruit and lemon to a makeshift mint julep. The ingredients are simple: flavored vodka, triple sec, fresh OJ (squeezed directly from the fruit into the glass; anything else is cheating), and a spritz from the soda gun to top it off, served in a tall glass over loads of crushed ice.

Harborside's Orange Crush
2 oz orange vodka (preferably Smirnoff)
2 oz triple sec (preferably La Quinta)
Juice of one navel orange, freshly squeezed
Lemon-lime soda to finish (preferably Sprite or Sierra Mist)

12841 Harbor Rd., Ocean City
410-213-1846
weocharborside.com

MEET NEW (OLD) FRIENDS IN EASTPORT
AT DAVIS' PUB

Every port needs a great sailors' bar, and in Annapolis, that's Davis' Pub. Located on Back Creek in Eastport, this 1920s general store has morphed into the perfect dive bar, with wood-paneled walls, a long bar area that's always packed with locals, and a tiny rear dining room. In the summer, the side patio opens up, almost doubling capacity. It may be a dive (with the restrooms to prove it), but the food is no joke. The cheesy crab-topped pretzels are utterly craveworthy, as are the crab dip–topped tater tots, and the BBQ sandwich has been featured on *Diners, Drive-ins and Dives*. If it seems like everyone knows each other, that's intentional; their slogan is "There are no strangers, only friends you haven't met yet."

400 Chester Ave.
410-268-7432
davispub.com

EAT IN THE STREET
AT DINNER UNDER THE STARS

What started as a way to lure people to upper West Street quickly turned into an Annapolis summertime tradition. Every Wednesday from late May through September, the first block of West Street between Church Circle and Calvert Street is closed to vehicular traffic and all of the restaurants bring tables out onto the brick-paved street, inviting wandering diners to stroll down and take a seat. The offerings are varied, from sushi and sake at Tsunami to tacos and tequila at El Toro Bravo. Strings of Edison lights overhead set the mood while a changing array of live bands keep bystanders dancing. Most restaurants operate on a first-come, first-served basis; if your pick has a wait, head inside one of the bars for a drink or amuse yourself with some great people watching.

Annapolis Arts District, 92 W. Washington St.
410-858-5884
dinnerunderthestars.org

GET CRAFTY
ON THE EASTERN SHORE

The Eastern Shore has contenders to rival craft breweries in any part of the country, but here are three of the best. Set in an airy former pool hall in Cambridge, RaR's Pulp Friction was named one of the top IPAs in the country by *Draft* magazine, and their new-brew releases get lines out the door. Evolution in Salisbury is a full-scale affair, with tasting room and brewery tours plus an adjacent public house open for lunch and dinner, and a bourbon barrel–aged Rise Up Russian Imperial Stout that gets top marks on BeerAdvocate.com. Burley Oak wins for looks, with their rustic barn setting and outdoor beer garden, and their tasty Lost Oak IPA is on tap around the state. These breweries are always experimenting, and friendly bartenders will lead you through tastings or make suggestions for your particular palate.

RaR Brewing, 504 Poplar St., Cambridge
443-225-5664
rarbrewing.com

Evolution Craft Brewing Co. & Public House
201 E. Vine St., Salisbury
443-260-2337
evolutioncraftbrewing.com

Burley Oak Brewing Company
10016 Old Ocean City Blvd., Berlin
443-513-4647
burleyoak.com

CELEBRATE IN GOOD TASTE
AT LEWNES' STEAKHOUSE

To me, nothing says special occasion like a classic steakhouse. And Lewnes' Steakhouse in Annapolis has all of the components of a great one: dry-aged steaks and chops; low-key, old-school service that makes you feel looked after but not rushed; bartenders who know how to make a killer martini or Manhattan; and loads of ambiance in the form of high-backed leather booths, wood-paneled walls, and black-and-white neighborhood photos. For a twist in tradition, start with the Greek salad, served in honor of family scion Sam Lewnes, who ran a corner store on this same spot back in the 1920s. The fact that the current restaurant is run by the fourth generation of the same family makes it even more special, whatever your occasion.

401 Fourth St.
410-263-1617
lewnessteakhouse.com

EAT UP IN EASTON

Easton's culinary scene is both exciting and easy, centered in its historic, walkable downtown. Hunters Tavern puts a modern take on regional ingredients with dishes like venison Bolognese, duck two ways, and snapping turtle soup. Out of the Fire makes magic with their stone-hearth oven and organic ingredients, evidenced by their wood-fired pizza topped with spinach, feta, and merguez sausage. Over at the BBQ Joint, competition chef Andrew Evans' hormone-free meats—brisket, pork, ribs, turkey and chicken—are smoked onsite and served wet or dry, with six bespoke sauce options. Scossa serves up authentic Northern Italian cuisine, courtesy of chef Giancarlo Tondin, who began his career at the legendary Harry's Bar in Venice. And I can't leave town without hitting up Piazza Italian Market for warm paninis, fresh pignoli cookies, and a smart selection of groceries imported from Italy.

Hunters Tavern, 101 E. Dover St.
410-822-4034, tidewaterinn.com/hunters-tavern

Out of the Fire, 22 Goldsborough St.
410-770-4777, outofthefire.com

The BBQ Joint, 216 E. Dover St.
410-690-3641, andrewevansbbqjoint.com

Scossa, 8 N. Washington St.
410-822-2202, scossarestaurant.com

Piazza Italian Market, 218 N. Washington St.
410-820-8281, piazzaitalianmarket.com

FOLLOW
THE CHESAPEAKE WINE TRAIL

The Chesapeake Bay region shares a similar climate to France's Loire Valley (albeit with saltier *terroir*), and the nascent wine industry puts out surprisingly tasty varietals. Here are three standout wineries to get you started.

Great Frogs Centered around a weathered, reclaimed tobacco barn, this working vineyard offers tasty wines in a rustic-chic setting. Due to popularity, tastings are done by appointment only, but visitors can buy wines by the glass or bottle at its myriad events, from live music to artisans' markets.

3218 Harness Creek Rd., Annapolis, 410-626-6193, greatfrogs.com

Chateau Bu-De Vineyard & Winery Located outside of Chesapeake City, this modern, barn-style winery features a horseshoe-shaped tasting bar, comfy lounge, and French doors that lead out to a large lawn and the river beyond.

237 Bohemia Manor Farm Ln., Chesapeake City, 410-885-2500, chateaubude.com

Bordeleau Vineyard & Winery Bordeleau is known for its cabernet sauvignon, which took gold at the Maryland Wine Awards. Bring your own picnic and make a day of it, tasting al fresco on the patio or down on the dock.

3155 Noble Farm Rd., Eden, 410-677-3334, bordeleauwine.com

BITE INTO BETTERTON
AT BARBARA'S ON THE BAY

One of my favorite Eastern Shore experiences is driving the rural roads that splinter off from Route 50—which is even more fun to do if you have a tasty destination as an excuse. The tiny town of Betterton (population, 350) was a resort enclave in the early 1900s, serving frolickers who came by steamboat from Baltimore to beat the heat. It's also where you'll find chef Barbara Esmonde. She trained in NYC under chef Bobby Flay and worked around the country before a chance encounter with a "For Rent" sign in Betterton inspired her to go out on her own. The aptly named Barbara's on the Bay is set in a cheery hillside cottage overlooking the beach, with big windows and a deck to embrace the view. Homestyle dishes like Maryland crab soup, shrimp and grits, and open-face crab cake melt suit the locale, and she makes the best Southern-style grilled oysters this side of Charleston.

12 Ericsson Ave., Betterton, 410-348-3079, barbarasonthebay.com

TIP
Make the most of your drive by spending the day at the beach. Inflow from the Sassafras River keeps the water clear and nettle-free, even in August, and the off-the-beaten-path location means there's always room to spread a towel.

SIP A CUPPA
AT REYNOLDS TAVERN

Built in 1747 as a haberdashery and "ordinary," Reynolds Tavern was a favorite meeting spot in the colonial era. (George Washington was known to party here back in the day, after attending horse races nearby.) It's still an ideal spot to enjoy that very English of traditions, afternoon tea. Take a seat in the Victorian-style dining room, marked with original wooden floors, linen-covered tables, and displays of vintage china, and you'll be presented with a selection of loose teas, along with a multi-tiered array of teatime classics: fresh-baked scones, crustless finger sandwiches, and a selection of tiny tarts and cakes to finish up. If you're in a celebratory mood, up the fun factor with a glass of sparking rosé. Tea not your thing? Head downstairs to the 1747 Pub, which was the tavern's original kitchen. It still oozes atmosphere with its low ceiling, brick floors, and stone fireplace. In warmer months, the backyard beer garden hosts events from concerts to movies under the stars.

7 Church Circle
410-295-9555
reynoldstavern.org

DINE ON TEA
IN ROYAL OAK

The town of Royal Oak is blink-and-you'll-miss-it small, but it makes a big mark on the dining scene thanks to T at the General Store. This eclectic eatery is set in an early-1900s general store that has been lovingly updated with a tin ceiling, cast-iron piping, and refreshed cabinetry. The *T* comes from the extensive menu of loose-leaf teas, tea-based cocktails, and tea-inspired dishes like chai-rubbed roasted chicken. The combination of tasty food and retro bistro ambiance draws diners from all across Talbot County and beyond. They're open for dinner all week and brunch on weekends. If you don't have a reservation, expect a wait in season. Happily, you can spend that time browsing the nooks and crannies of Oak Creek Sales antique store across the street.

25942 Royal Oak Rd., Easton
410-745-8402
tatthegeneralstore.com

EMBRACE THE VIEW
FROM A HARBOR-SIDE TABLE

One surprising thing about downtown Annapolis is that, despite it being a harbor town, there aren't many restaurants where you can sit outside and dine right by the water, rather than across the street from it. Set on the Eastport side of Spa Creek, directly above the Pier 4 Marina, Carrol's Creek Cafe has a great outdoor deck overlooking the harbor and historic City Dock beyond, making it a top spot for locals and visitors alike. And the food is as good as the view; don't miss the show-stopping scallops, served in nests of shredded phyllo over lump crab and wilted spinach, and the local rockfish smothered in lump crab and beurre blanc.

For something more casual, check out Pusser's Caribbean Grille, which edges Ego Alley and overlooks City Dock. This spot shines at happy hour, when crowds gather for drink specials and live acoustic music as they watch pleasure boats maneuver their way down the channel and back.

Carrol's Creek Cafe, 410 Severn Ave.
410-263-8012
carrolscreek.com

Pusser's Caribbean Grille, 80 Compromise St.
410-626-0004
pussersannapolis.com

GET SPIRITED
DOWNEE OCEAN

Going "downee ocean" is a rite of passage for college kids, and Ocean City has the throngs of drinking establishment to prove it. Seacrets is by far the biggest, with eighteen bars, a sand beach, multiple stages, and a massive nightclub. If rowdy parties and dance music aren't your thing, head to Seacrets Distillery next door. The first distillery to open in Wicomico County since the end of Prohibition, they produce award-winning spirits in a speakeasy-style setting stocked with nearly one million dollars' worth of Prohibition-era antiques, including an Edison Labs workbench, a 1920s phone booth, and an original 1927 Tommy Gun. The tour begins as you punch in at the vintage timeclock, takes you through the distilling process, and ends with password-only entry into the tasting room for three samples of your choice. I like the spiced rum and orange vodka, but you can't go wrong with any—and you can buy discounted bottles to go in the onsite gift shop.

Seacrets Distillery, 117 49th St., Ocean City
410-524-2669
seacretsdistilling.com

SAMPLE A FOOD HALL
AT MARKET HOUSE

The market house at Annapolis's City Dock has seen a lot of changes in its 160 years, with incarnations as grocery store, takeout spot and even empty relic for ten years, post Tropical Storm Isabel in 2003. But the food hall that stands there now is the best version yet, in my opinion. In the light-filled, warehouse space, a long open kitchen prepares made-to-order options like paninis, flatbreads, and burgers, as well as tasty grain bowls with ingredients including farro and ahi tuna. Enjoy them at communal tables or the long counter overlooking Ego Alley, which is a great spot for people watching. Evening has a whole different vibe, as diners cluster around the oyster bar for fresh shellfish and crudos paired with a robust list of wines and craft beer. You can pass the time with their array of loaner board games, or get something to go if you're in a rush.

25 Market Space
443-949-0024
annapolismarkethouse.com

GET AN EARFUL
ON THE EASTERN SHORE

Summer just isn't summer without fresh Eastern Shore sweet corn. You'll find it at farmer's markets across the Shore, along with tomatoes, string beans, peaches, cantaloupes, and every other kind of produce you can imagine, fed by this fertile soil. Acclaimed Easton chef Jordan Lloyd swears by Taylor's Produce for the sweetest corn, available at six regional produce stands, including St. Michaels, Oxford, and the largest near their farm in Preston. Over on Route 50, just outside Salisbury, the Wright family vends produce grown on 650 acres at their four-generation family farm, along with all manner of goods from jam and baked goodies to Amish-style wooden furniture. Take time to feed the resident goats, who are as cute as the strawberry pie is delicious.

Taylor's Produce, 22816 Dover Bridge Rd., Preston
443-786-1296
taylorsproduce.com

Wright's Market, 9300 Old Railroad Rd., Mardela Springs
410-742-8845
wrightsmarket.com

TRY
A TIN OR TOAST
AT SAILOR OYSTER BAR

Oh, how I love Sailor Oyster Bar! The menu is simple yet eclectic. Start with fresh-shucked oysters, spanning from local waters to the Pacific Northwest and served on freshly shaved ice with handmade mignonette, cocktail, and hot sauces. The lobster toast—featuring Maine meat accented with sea salt—is thoroughly craveworthy. Imported tinned fish comes packed in olive oil and served with artisanal bread, salted butter, and baby arugula as a DIY spread. Tasty craft cocktails are divvied up by strength (light, medium, and strong) and complemented by a well-curated selection of wine and craft beer. Whether you're a regular or a first-timer dining solo, the waitstaff is unfailingly welcoming and knowledgeable enough to make you want to try new things. (Even tinned fish!) The natty, striped-shirt uniforms and retro sailor pinup art are a cheeky nod to Annapolis's nautical ties and the perfect finishing touch.

196 West St.
410-571-5449
sailoroysterbar.com

GET TO THE POINT
AT THE POINT CRAB HOUSE

Ok, so The Point is technically upstream in Arnold, but it feels quintessentially Annapolis. Set in a working marina just off the Magothy River, this tin-roofed former warehouse has an airy, open interior, with floor-to-ceiling, garage-style windows that roll up on three sides in summer, better to take in the water breezes. They offer steamed crabs in season, best enjoyed at picnic tables on the patio. But any time of year you can dig into crab dip served with warm pretzel bread, tasty steamed shrimp or ahi tuna tacos, and my favorite, deviled eggs topped with jumbo lump crab. They have a loyal neighborhood crowd all year long, but it gets even more popular in warmer months, with a wait to get in. It's worth it.

700 Mill Creek Rd., Arnold
410-544-5448
thepointcrabhouse.com

TIP
Wednesday nights bring live music and half-priced bottles of house wine—the perfect recipe for a mid-week wind-down.

BET
ON THE BOOZE TRIFECTA

Craft booze is all the rage, but nowhere are producers as conveniently situated as in St. Michaels, with four within a single city block. Start off at Lyon Distilling Company's micro distillery, which offers tours and tastes of their stellar rums and whiskeys. Sharing the same space is Gray Wolf Craft Distilling, whose tasty Timber Sassafras gin is infused with cardamom, peppercorn, and hibiscus. Next, head a few steps over to St. Michaels Winery, which offers dollar samples of eighteen varietals. End your tour at friendly Eastern Shore Brewing; the oldest microbrewery on the Eastern Shore, they've won state awards for their Back Creek Blonde ale. The brewery is part tasting room (they have ten brews on tap, plus cans and growlers to go), and part neighborhood hangout with darts, tabletop shuffleboard, and live music.

Lyon Distilling Company, 605 S. Talbot St.
443-333-9181, lyondistilling.com

Gray Wolf Craft Distilling, 605 S. Talbot St.
443-339-4894, graywolfcraftdistilling.com

St. Michaels Winery, 609 S. Talbot St.
410-745-0808, st-michaels-winery.com

Eastern Shore Brewing, 605 S. Talbot St.
410-745-8010, easternshorebrewing.com

HAVE A REUNION
AT MCGARVEY'S SALOON
AND OYSTER BAR

If there's one bar that's synonymous with Annapolis and the Naval Academy, it would be McGarvey's. As my brother Pat, a USNA graduate, says, "If I ever want to see who's in town, I just go down to McGarvey's and see who I run into." The site has been a bar since 1871, but its current reputation was built by owner Mike Ashford, who ran it for forty years. The loyal following is due in equal parts to the convivial staff, quality food (try the roast beef hash or anything from the raw bar), and prime location just two blocks from the Academy's main gate. When Ashford sold the bar in 2016, it was to three former midshipmen who promised to keep everything exactly the same, from the Aviator lager on tap to the donated flight helmets displayed behind the bar. I like the front room best, especially in the afternoon when the wooden bar gleams with filtered sunlight and the evening crowds haven't yet descended. Pat's partial to the sunroom, where a live tree grows up toward the skylight. I've been there for brunch, for lunch, and in the wee hours—and almost every time I happily run into someone I haven't seen in ages. That's just how it goes at McGarvey's.

8 Market Space
410-263-5700
mcgarveysannapolis.com

· · · · · · · · · · · · · · · · · · · ·

WATCH THE WORLD GO BY
AT THE BIG OWL TIKI BAR

Kent Narrows is a skinny channel separating Kent Island from the Delmarva Peninsula. The waterway is a popular pass-through for boats running around the Bay, and the bridge spanning it is part of Route 50, the main highway connecting Ocean City to Washington, D.C. The Big Owl Tiki Bar is perched front and center on the channel just south of the bridge, an ideal position for watching all the comings and goings. Walking down the wooden pier to the floating bar feels like strolling into vacation mode, a feeling that's amplified when you grab a dockside stool and order up gin and tonics paired with rockfish tenders or garlic butter clams. I like Big Owl best on summer Sunday afternoons when the pleasure boats are out en masse and the backed-up traffic headed back from the beach to DC makes me grateful I have no other place to be.

3015 Kent Narrow Way S, Grasonville
410-827-6523
thebigowl.com

FEAST WITH 2,500 FRIENDS
AT THE ROTARY CRAB FEAST

By sheer numbers alone, the area's biggest party has to be the Rotary Crab Feast, a charity fundraiser held every August in the parking lot of Navy–Marine Corps Memorial Stadium in Annapolis. Each year, up to twenty-five hundred people line up in the afternoon to enter the tents at five o'clock, where they settle in at long, butcher paper–covered tables for three hours of all-you-can-eat steamed crabs, vats of crab soup, local sweet corn on the cob, plus barbecue, hot dogs, and trimmings, all washed down with soda and beer. It's billed as the largest crab feast in the world, and who am I to argue? The event goes on rain or shine, as it's been doing since 1946, and all proceeds go to local charities.

annapolisrotary.org

TIP
In partnership with Annapolis Green, a local nonprofit, all paper products and trash are recycled, and the organic waste (crab shells, corn cobs, etc.) is gathered and recycled into area gardens as "Crab Compost" come fall.

REDISCOVER ICE CREAM
AT SCOTTISH HIGHLAND CREAMERY

You may think you've had good ice cream in the past, but if you haven't tasted the frozen goods at Scottish Highland Creamery, you really haven't. First, they painstakingly source the best ingredients, be it the freshest possible cream or flavored extracts imported from Italy. Each batch is made onsite, by hand, one gallon at a time, from blending the sugar and cream to baking the cake that goes into their Birthday Cake flavor. The result is a surprisingly creative output, with a product range spanning six hundred variations that change out by season or whim. At least sixteen flavors are offered onsite, with flavors changing multiple times per day as one sells out and is replaced by something different. The shop is only open from April through October; if you need to get your fix off-season, pick up a gallon at Oxford Social Cafe in Oxford, Town & Country Liquors in Easton, or Tilghman Island Country Store on Tilghman Island.

314 Tilghman St., Oxford
410-924-6298
scottishhighlandcreamery.com

TIP

Every July, the creamery holds their Ice Cream for Breakfast event. Patrons line up well before the doors open at 8:30 am to get their hands on custom flavors like Blueberry Muffin or Maple Syrup. (The latter typically sells out within the first hour.)

The Ram's Head Tavern

MUSIC AND ENTERTAINMENT

TUNE IN
AT RAMS HEAD TAVERN

With a thriving independent radio station (WRNR) and live music somewhere every night of the week, Annapolis is a great music town, and Rams Head Tavern is the crown jewel of the music scene. What started thirty years ago as a tiny basement pub is now a veritable empire, with four locations across the region. But the ultimate showcase is Rams Head On Stage in Annapolis, which features nationally renowned performers almost every night. You might see a cool indie band one night, a songwriting legend like Kris Kristofferson the next. The sit-down theater accommodates 312 people, giving each show a uniquely intimate feel. And performers love this venue as much as the audience does, building it into tour after tour. Waitstaff serves light fare (apps, sandwiches and flatbreads) and drinks during a show, or you can do a pre- or post-show dinner in the warren of cozy, brick-walled dining rooms that make up the restaurant; there's also an open-air beer garden in warmer months. The smaller Tavern stage hosts local acts most nights, typically Americana or roots-based.

33 West St.
410-268-4545
ramsheadonstage.com

TIP

That original basement pub is still there,
tucked under the larger Tavern. With its
centuries-old brick walls, timber ceiling, and
cozy fireplace, it's one of the best spots
in town for a nightcap whether you saw
a show upstairs or not.

CELEBRATE SUMMER ON STAGE
AT THE SUMMER GARDEN THEATRE

Theater under the stars is a summertime tradition in Annapolis, thanks to Summer Garden Theatre. Set in a restored nineteenth-century, brick-and-frame warehouse across from City Dock, this is community theater at its best, run on the power of volunteers, from the actors and crew to the ushers and office staff. The company was founded in 1966, and generations of Annapolitans have grown up performing in, supporting, or attending these shows, which run every weekend from Memorial Day to Labor Day. The program focuses on musicals, with an eye toward blending new works with crowd-pleasers. The theater is open-air, and the show goes on whatever the weather, be it rain or steamy August heat. That's part of the experience, as is intermission, when the crowd spills out on the street, their enthusiasm encouraging passers-by to buy their own tickets to an upcoming show.

143 Compromise St.
410-268-9212
summergarden.com

COME ALONG
TO THE AVALON

This gem of a theater in Easton originally opened in 1922, wowing vaudeville audiences with its leaded glass doors, eighteen-foot dome, and electric-pneumatic pipe organ. In the 1930s, it morphed into a movie theater, premiering films by Gary Cooper and Bette Davis. But times changed, and in the 1980s it closed for a number of years. Enter the city of Easton, which bought it at auction in 1989, and the Avalon Foundation, which now runs it as a nonprofit theater. A loving renovation restored its beauty, reclaiming its position as artistic hub for the Mid Shore. The main theater seats four hundred in an Art Deco backdrop of hand-painted gilt-and-red accents and stained-glass skylights under the still-intact dome. Or cozy up in the sixty-seat Stoltz Listening Room, a black-box, cabaret-style theater. Whatever your preferred entertainment, Avalon likely has it; they host national touring acts playing anything from jazz to bluegrass, plus regional bands and singer-songwriters, a children's theater, and live-broadcast opera from the Met.

40 E. Dover St., Easton
410-822-7299
avalonfoundation.org

LISTEN ON THE LAWN
AT TIDES & TUNES

One of my favorite ways to spend a summer Thursday is at the Annapolis Maritime Museum's annual music series, Tides & Tunes. Judging from the crowds, I'm not alone. From mid-June through mid-August, local bands take over an outdoor stage set up on the side of the museum, overlooking Back Creek. A festive throng fills the surrounding grassy space with blankets, lawn chairs, kids, and dogs, and the overflow spills onto the nearby docks, creating an only-in-Annapolis evening. Add in a cash bar and snacks from food trucks, and you have all the makings of a perfect summer night. Concerts showcase everything from folk to rock to reggae, with the biggest turnout for local sons, Eastport Oyster Boys, whose folk-inspired songs of Chesapeake Bay life go hand in hand with the waterfront setting. Come September, the event moves to Ellen O. Moyer Nature Park for another month as the September Sunsets concert series. Admission is always free, but donations are gladly accepted. Proceeds from bar sales benefit the museum.

Annapolis Maritime Museum, 723 Second St.
410-295-0104
amaritime.org

MASTER THE ARTS
AT MARYLAND HALL

It's hard to wrap your head around everything that goes on at Maryland Hall for the Creative Arts, a former high school that's the centerpiece of all things artistic in Anne Arundel County. It's home to the Annapolis Symphony Orchestra, Annapolis Opera, Annapolis Chorale, and Ballet Theatre of Maryland, all of whom perform there throughout the year. The auditorium also hosts concerts that need more space than nearby clubs can supply, whether it be the legendary Temptations or consummate jazz bandleader Chris Botti. Four gallery spaces offer rotating exhibits of painting, photography, sculpture, and experiential installations, attracting large crowds on opening nights. And a full slate of classes for kids and adults is available on everything from ceramics to digital editing. If you're arts inclined, whatever the medium, they'll have something to inspire you.

801 Chase St.
410-263-5544
marylandhall.org

GET CLASSICAL
ON CHURCH CIRCLE

Perched on the second-highest point of land in downtown Annapolis, St. Anne's is the city's oldest parish, with a history that dates back to the late 1600s. The circa-1859, Romanesque-style church is actually the third St. Anne's building; the first two were lost to expansion and fire, respectively. Inside are unique features such as a brass lectern from the Confederate ship *C.S.S. Shenandoah*, a Tiffany stained-glass window, and charming handmade needlepoint kneelers in the pews, each one unique and made by a parishioner. Take it all in during the St. Anne's Concert Series, which runs Thursday evenings in the spring and fall, showcasing everything from Bach to opera to contemporary Broadway showtunes. The annual December performances of Handel's *Messiah*—in conjunction with Maryland Hall for the Creative Arts, Annapolis Chorale, and Annapolis Chamber Orchestra—are a holiday tradition, extraordinarily moving to experience in a place with such simple beauty.

Church Circle
410-267-9333
stannes-annapolis.org

SING WITH THE PIANO MAN
AT MIDDLETON TAVERN

It's nine o'clock on a Saturday (or a Friday) and the regular crowd (plus some out-of-towners) shuffles in. They're coming to see Larry Lay, who has been playing sing-alongs in the upstairs room at Middleton Tavern for nearly twenty-five years. His playlist runs the gamut from Elton John to Frank Sinatra to Nirvana, and the rowdy crowd sings along at the top of their lungs. Not into piano bars? You can catch live bands most weekends in the downstairs pub. And what a pub it is! Middleton's was established as an "inn for seafaring men" back in 1750, and in the revolutionary era it played host to non-seafaring celebrities including Benjamin Franklin and George Washington. The well-designed back bar has plenty of seats, but I like to get a table in the downstairs dining room, cozy with wood-paneled walls and a blazing fire in the centuries-old brick fireplace.

2 Market Space
410-263-3323
middletontavern.com

SET THE STAGE
WITH THE COLONIAL PLAYERS

Founded in 1949, The Colonial Players is the oldest-running community theater in Annapolis. But don't let the name fool you; it comes from their location in the colonial capital, not the slant of their play selection. The 180-seat theater puts on seven shows per season: one musical, one holiday show, and five plays. The schedule can include anything from a Neil Simon classic to lesser-known works like 2018's "Silent Sky," which told the story of circa-1900 female astronomers. All shows are presented in the round, which leads to creative staging and an up-close experience for attendees. Their theater may be small, but the troupe has a big regional presence, consistently winning awards from the Washington Area Theatre Community Honors.

108 East St.
410-268-7373
thecolonialplayers.org

TIP
You can purchase tickets per show or subscribe annually with seats to each play. But my favorite way to go is with the FlexTicket, which gets you ten discounted seats to spread out however you wish throughout the season.

SEE HOW A GUITAR IS BORN
AT PAUL REED SMITH GUITARS

When a teenaged Paul Smith began building instruments from scratch back in the mid-1970s, no one imagined what his passion would lead to. But today, the Kent Island–based Paul Reed Smith Guitars is one of the premier guitar companies in the world, with a waiting list of up to six months for custom instruments. The free factory tour, held twice weekly, takes you out onto the factory floor to witness the process from start to finish: choosing the wood, cutting and pressing the tops and bottoms, designing the head stocks and mother-of-pearl inlays, and hand-staining each piece in layers to create a beautiful hue and shine. Even if you're not a guitar player or enthusiast (though most people who take it are both), the tour is fascinating.

380 Log Canoe Circle, Stevensville
410-643-9970
prsguitars.com

HUM ALONG
WITH THE USNA GLEE CLUB

The U.S. Naval Academy's mission is to train the next generation of naval officers, but they also have an incredible music department. The Men's and Women's Glee Clubs are the headline attraction. Their annual performance of Handel's *Messiah* at the USNA Chapel, in conjunction with the Annapolis Symphony and Annapolis Opera, is always a sell-out and broadcast nationally on PBS. You can also catch them live every fall during Parents' Weekend and at their Spring Oratorio every March at Maryland Hall for the Creative Arts, backed by the Annapolis Symphony Orchestra. For something lighter, book tickets for their annual musical, always a full-on Broadway-style production with a live pit orchestra.

US Naval Academy Musical Activities Department
410-293-2439
usna.edu/music

TIP
If you can only see one event, make it the annual Halloween Concert, a two-night, over-the-top spectacle of laser-light show, dramatic costumes, and organ-backed music performed for a sell-out crowd at the USNA Chapel.

MEET THE MASTERS
AT ANNAPOLIS SYMPHONY ORCHESTRA

The Annapolis Symphony Orchestra started casually in 1961, when a few amateur musicians began practicing during their lunch hour, just for the love of playing. As word got out, the group expanded, and now ASO is the largest performing arts group in Anne Arundel County. An ensemble of seventy professional musicians, led by conductor José-Luis Novo, perform multiple concerts throughout the year, often joined by internationally acclaimed guest musicians such as violinist MidoriGotō, guitarist Manuel Barrueco, and pianist Pascal Rogé. Most concerts are held at Maryland Hall for the Creative Arts, and the ever-changing program ranges from great composers and collaborations with the USNA Glee Club to live performances playing along with silent films.

801 Chase St., Suite 204
410-269-1132
annapolissymphony.org

TIP
Cap off the summer season with the annual Pops in the Park at Quiet Waters Park. The concert is free, but you'll want to get there early to claim space for your blanket, lawn chairs, and picnic basket.

HAVE A GOOD *CRAIC*
AT GALWAY BAY

Craic is the Irish term for a certain kind of good time, accented with lively banter, good friends and probably music. And that's what usually ends up happening at Galway Bay, a quintessential Irish pub in Annapolis. The vibe is intentionally convivial, with no TVs to distract from the art of conversation. Bartenders greet you like a friend, and a visit typically ends with newfound pals gabbing over anything from local news to their Irish ancestors—in other words, a mighty *craic*. Wednesday nights bring a traditional Irish jam session, with regulars on button accordion, banjo, and fiddle, plus other players dropping in. On Sunday afternoons, a singer on acoustic guitar eases you through the waning weekend hours. The restaurant is one of the best in town, with shepherd's pie, lamb stew, and an all-day Irish breakfast, while the bar offers Guinness on draft (along with local craft brews) and the largest selection of whiskeys in Maryland.

63 Maryland Ave.
410-263-8333
galwaybaymd.com

CONNECT OVER COFFEE
AT 49 WEST

In the United States, coffee shops are mainly about coffee. But in Europe, they're designed as social centers—places to linger for inspiration, conversation, and kinship. That's the idea behind 49 West in Annapolis. Yes, there's coffee by day, and you can always find people reading, working on laptops, or quietly chatting over salads or sandwiches. But you'll also find curated exhibits by local artists and live music pretty much every night of the week. The front room tends towards acoustic, be it singer-songwriters in the early evening or samba for Sunday brunch. But the tiny back room is the secret gem; with experimental jazz one night and bluegrass the next, you never know what you're going to find. Regardless of what's on, there's always something to make you feel, think, and connect—and that's exactly the point.

49 West St.
410-626-9796
49westcoffeehouse.com

SCARE YOURSELF SILLY
ON A GHOST TOUR

Ghost tours are a great way to learn more about a town's past and its present, with tales of recent specter sightings. And with four hundred years of history, Annapolis is fertile ground for hauntings. Annapolis Ghost Tours & Crawls offers a year-round slate of walking tours that take you down cobblestone streets, into haunted cemeteries, and past historic buildings hiding ghastly secrets, like the landmark Georgian home where midnight wails have been heard in the wee hours. For something lighter, the Haunted Pub Crawl is a fun twist on the traditional, taking you into historic taverns for drinks and stories.

On the Eastern Shore, no one knows hauntings better than Mindie Burgoyne. Her company, Chesapeake Ghost Tours, offers a dozen deeply researched tours in towns from Berlin to St. Michaels, in what she calls the largest cluster of heritage ghost tours in the United States. They also offer bus tours that cover more ground than a walking tour, introducing you to local legends like Big Lizz, a murdered slave who beckons the living into Greenbriar Swamp, where they are never seen again.

Annapolis Ghost Tours & Crawls, 13 Francis St.
443-534-0043, toursandcrawls.com

Chesapeake Ghost Tours, 5775 Charles Cannon Rd., Marion Station
443-735-0771, chesapeakeghosts.com

PLAY AROUND
AT THE PRINCE

Home to Washington College, Chestertown has a robust cultural scene exceeding its small size. Much of the action takes place in the Jazz Age–era Prince Theatre. Built as a movie theater in the waning days of silent films, it operated as a family-owned movie house until it closed in 1993. Local visionaries rehabbed and opened it in 2002 as home to the Garfield Center for the Arts. The bilevel theater features a deep stage accented by a *trompe l'oeil* archway, with flexible seating for up to 220. The resident community troupe puts on four top-quality plays per year, and the theater hosts myriad events, from improv and open mics to the Live Playwrights' Society for Play Writers, Readers, Observers & Critics, where writers share samples of their work in an open, encouraging forum.

210 High St., Chestertown
410-810-2060
garfieldcenter.org

TIP
Want a fast culture fix? Check out the Short Attention Span Theater, a two-week-long festival showcasing ten-minute plays.

SPORTS AND RECREATION

WALK THE BRIDGE
ACROSS THE BAY

The Chesapeake Bay Bridge was the longest over-water steel structure in the world when it was built, stretching 4.3 miles from Sandy Point to Kent Island. But unlike other famous spans, such as Brooklyn or Golden Gate, this bridge is for vehicles only—except for one day every May, when runners and walkers take it over as part of the Across the Bay 10K. Up to twenty-five thousand enthusiasts register for the 6.6-mile race, which starts at Sandy Point State Park, heads over the eastbound span, and finishes at Queen Anne's Park. Not a regular runner? No worries; an estimated 30 percent of participants have never done a 10K before and sign up mostly to enjoy the view of sailboat-dotted waters from two hundred feet up. That said, this isn't a sightseeing stroll; the pace is intentionally kept brisk, and stopping for photos is verboten—as are selfie sticks.

Across the Bay 10K
acrossthebridge10K.com

TIP

Due to its length, height, and low, open guard rails, the dual-span bridge has been named one of the scariest spans in the country. Kent Island Express offers drive-over service for thirty-five dollars each way—the perfect solution for gephyrophobes.

325 Log Canoe Circle, Stevensville
410-604-0486
kentislandexpress.com

WATCH THE WEDNESDAY RACES
AT CITY DOCK

The Wednesday Night Races have been an Annapolis tradition since 1959. More than one hundred boats compete in the weekly regatta, which runs from May through August. The action starts around half past four at City Dock, as competing boats ready their sails at downtown marinas or sail in from Spa Creek, skillfully tacking back and forth in the crowded harbor as they wait for the six-o'clock starting gun. Much of the regatta takes place out on the Bay, around a buoy-marked course, before ending at the finish line at Annapolis Yacht Club. A chase boat and video crew films all of the action on the water, replaying it later that evening at the members-only Annapolis Yacht Club and at the public Boatyard Bar & Grill, the top spot for post-race frivolity.

Annapolis Yacht Club, 2 Compromise St.
410-263-9279
annapolisyc.com

Boatyard Bar & Grill, 400 Fourth St.
410-216-6206
boatyardbarandgrill.com

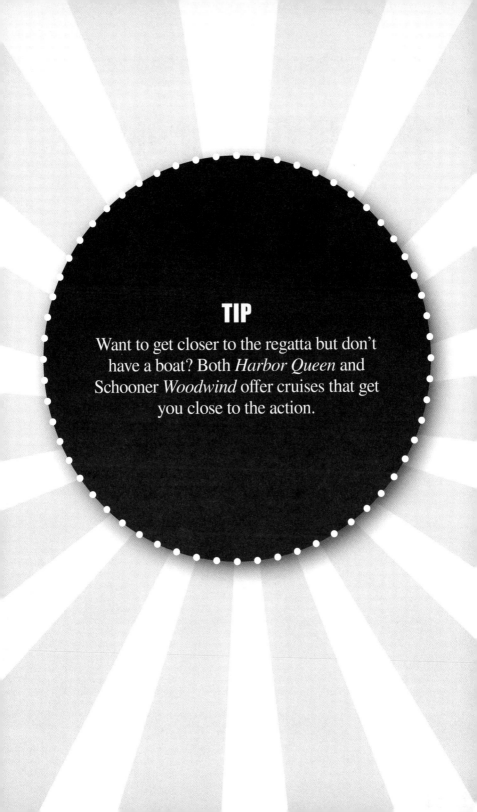

TIP

Want to get closer to the regatta but don't have a boat? Both *Harbor Queen* and Schooner *Woodwind* offer cruises that get you close to the action.

PADDLE THE POCOMOKE
ON THE EASTERN SHORE

The Eastern Shore is filled with beautiful rivers, but none are prettier than the Pocomoke, the region's easternmost tributary. This narrow, deep river passes through a southern gothic landscape edged by the country's northernmost stands of cypress. Tannins from the trees give the river its dark appearance, and the depth (up to forty-five feet) makes it brilliantly reflective. Taking to the tributary is like going back in time, with turtles nosing up for air between the lily pads and myriad types of warblers singing in the trees as you paddle the seemingly currentless water. Keep an eye out for nesting bald eagles, and you may even luck out with a river otter sighting. Pocomoke River Canoe in Snow Hill rents canoes, kayaks, and stand-up paddleboards and also offers drop-off/pick-up portage service from popular access points.

Pocomoke River Canoe Company, 2 River St., Snow Hill
410-632-3971
pocomokeriverpaddle.com

CHEER THE GOAT
AT A NAVY GAME

The U.S. Naval Academy brings its own traditions to football game day. Of course, there's tailgating, as alumni clubs set up elaborate party tents in the parking lot of the thirty-four-thousand-seat Navy–Marine Corps Memorial Stadium. The marching Drum & Bugle Corps makes its way through the gatherings, getting the crowd dancing to anything from "Hey Baby" to "Anchors Aweigh." As kickoff approaches, the forty-four-hundred-strong Brigade of Midshipmen parades onto the field in a tight formation called "March On," then stands company by company through the presentation of colors, national anthem, and a fly-over by Navy jets. Each time Navy scores during the game, a cannon is fired and the plebes (freshman) rush to the end zone, doing a push-up for each point on the scoreboard. Mascot Bill the Goat (a live goat, who lives his life under strict security to prevent kidnapping by rivals) is always on hand, placidly chewing grass on the sidelines as he unwittingly inspires the team to victory.

USNA football, navysports.com

TIP
If you don't have a tailgate invite, join the Captain's BBQ, where forty-two dollars gets you all you can eat and drink, supplied by a rotating cadre of local restaurants.

CRUISE TO ST. MICHAELS
WITH WATERMARK

Watermark Cruises offers dozens of boat tours in Annapolis and Baltimore, including Severn River runs aboard the genteel *Harbor Queen*, which moors at City Dock. But my favorite experience is their Day on the Bay cruise, which sails from Annapolis to historic St. Michaels—hands-down the most charming port on the Bay, especially when you arrive by water. After enjoying a two-and-one-half-hour morning cruise across the Bay (along with free coffee and donuts), spend the day exploring the Chesapeake Bay Maritime Museum (admission is included) and lunching or shopping downtown before reboarding the boat for the sunset trip home. There's no driving and no bridge traffic—and you can even bring your dog. St. Michaels sails run every Saturday and some weekdays throughout the summer, with extra boats added for special events like the St. Michaels Winefest.

410-268-7601
cruisesonthebay.com

TIP

Rock 'N River Cruises, done in
conjunction with WRNR, are held three
to four times each summer, with floating
performances by nationally renowned bands;
past years have brought in Anderson East
and The Record Company. It's always a
great time, and the shows sell out within
hours of being announced.

WALK IN THE WOODS
AT ADKINS ARBORETUM

The Adkins Arboretum is a secret treasure tucked inside Tuckahoe State Park. More than six hundred species of native trees, grasses, and flowers grow in the four-hundred-acre preserve, which is open daily from dawn to dusk. Start at the visitor center to find out what's in bloom, then head out to explore via five miles of walking paths that take you through silvery beech groves; over low, marsh-spanning bridges; and across wildflower-filled meadows. Hour-long, docent-led tours are offered every Saturday morning at ten o'clock, but the well-marked trails are a pleasure to wander at will, with signage highlighting anything from swamp milkweed to show-stopping dogwoods. The grounds are dog friendly, but please keep your pet leashed so as not to disturb resident wildlife, which include deer, foxes, and beavers.

12610 Eveland Rd., Ridgely
410-634-2847
adkinsarboretum.com

TIP
If you want a longer hike, the arboretum connects with the state park's trail system, adding another twenty miles of hiking and biking trails.

CATCH A CANOE RACE
AT THE GOVERNOR'S CUP

Log canoe sailing is a uniquely Chesapeake sport. The boats are crafted from joined logs, hollowed out to make a single shallow hull. An oversized mast—sometimes twice as high as the boat is long—is added for maximum sail size and maximum speed. The problem (or the appeal, depending on your take) is that the overwhelming weight of the mast and the lack of ballast makes the vessels extremely tippy. To compensate, the boats add long, plank-like "hiking boards" that extend horizontally out over the water; when underway, crews jam as many sailors as they can on the rails to counterbalance the weight of the sail. This actually works great— except when the wind shifts and the boat tips, throwing everyone into the drink!

Log canoe racers hold a series of summer regattas around the Bay, but the premiere event is the Governor's Cup, held every July by the Miles River Yacht Club in St. Michaels.

Governor's Cup Log Canoe Race, Miles River Yacht Club
24750 Yacht Club Rd., St. Michaels
410-745-9511, milesriveryc.com

TIP
If you want to see the races from sea, not shore, the Chesapeake Bay Maritime Museum's buyboat *Winnie Estelle* takes voyeurs as close to the action as they can get.

ENJOY SUNSET UNDER SAIL
ON SCHOONER *WOODWIND*

Annapolis is the sailing capital of the country, and no one offers a better sail than Schooner *Woodwind*, which operates twin seventy-four-foot clipper ships out of their berth at City Dock. The purpose-built boats are designed for an easy, relaxed ride, with plenty of deck space for taking in the Bay views. On the two-hour sunset sails, which run April through October, she heads out of Annapolis Harbor at five o'clock, bound for the Severn River and the Bay Bridge beyond. While underway, the captain shares stories of regional history and maritime landmarks, and the crew serves up craft beer and wine when they're not working the sails. The whole thing feels like being out with friends, and it's over way too soon. Luckily, they offer a frequent-sailing card, and you can earn free sails over the lifetime of the card.

80 Compromise St.
410-263-7837
schoonerwoodwind.com

TIP

Get your heart racing mid-week, when *Woodwind I* and *II* race each other as part of the Wednesday Night sailboat races. Not only do you get an up-close view of the regatta, but you get to feel the power of a clipper pushed to her limits under the hands of an expert crew.

WITNESS A REBIRTH
ON POPLAR ISLAND

Poplar Island has a fascinating history that belies its tiny size. English colonists settled here in the 1630s, it was a base for the British in the War of 1812, and in the 1930s it was home to a hunting club visited by U.S. presidents. But erosion and rising sea levels took their toll, shrinking the island from eleven hundred acres in 1847 to just four acres of marshy islets by the mid-1990s. Enter Maryland Environmental Services, which undertook the ambitious project to rebuild the isle with earth dredged from the neighboring channel, restoring habitat without damaging existing wildlife. The effort has been a roaring success, and the still-expanding island has become a refuge for migratory birds. The diamondback terrapin also thrives here, away from mainland predators.

Maryland Environmental Services offers three-hour tours, departing via boat weekday mornings from Tilghman Island from March through October. It's fascinating to see the juxtaposition of modern engineering and natural wonderland as herons, egrets, and ospreys go about their business amid massive working bulldozers and cranes from the Army Corps of Engineers. Work is due to go on for another thirty years; when it's finished, all traces of work will be removed, leaving the island as a nature sanctuary.

410-729-8200
poplarislandrestoration.com

BIKE ACROSS AN ISLAND
ON CROSS ISLAND TRAIL

Just across the Bay Bridge from Annapolis, Kent Island is one of the best places to explore on two wheels, due in equal parts to the flat landscape and stunning vistas. The purpose-built Cross Island Trail follows the footprint of the vanished Queen Anne's Railroad, which once ran the length of the island. Start at the easternmost point, Terrapin Nature Park, for amazing views of the Bay Bridge, then head west. The wide, paved path runs for 5.8 miles through open farmland and shady pine forest; multiple bridges along the way offer great water views in both directions. The trail ends at Ferry Point Park, where a boardwalk extends out over the marsh to a beach beyond. If you've worked up an appetite, numerous restaurants on both sides of Route 50 will sate you with fresh seafood and libations.

Terrapin Nature Area, Stevensville
410-758-0835, traillink.com/trail/cross-island-trail

TIP
If you want a longer ride, turn south on Route 8 near Terrapin State Park and head to the Matapeake Fishing Pier, where you can connect with the Kent Island South Trail for an additional six miles.

TAKE REFUGE IN NATURE
AT BLACKWATER REFUGE

People aren't the only ones who find the Eastern Shore so appealing. Countless flocks of waterfowl stop here on the annual migratory route known as the Atlantic Flyway, attracted by the twenty-seven-thousand-acre Blackwater National Wildlife Refuge. Each season has its own visitors. In December and January, snow geese and tundra swans arrive by the thousands, shimmering over the marshes like kinetic art installations. Spring brings migrating marsh and song birds, including green winged teal and bright yellow warblers. In summer, baby ospreys and eagles test their wings while white-tail fawns scamper in the marshland below. Year-round residents include bald eagles, great horned owls, and the once-endangered Delmarva Peninsula fox squirrel.

There are myriad ways to explore, with hiking trails and a drivable auto route that stops at different viewing platforms. My favorite way to go is by kayak, seeing the marshes at eye level like the birds do. Blackwater Adventures rents watercraft and offers guided tours, searching out spots where wildfowl gather. But even without wildlife sightings, the scenery is mesmerizing, with delicate wetland hues constantly shifting as the sun moves overhead.

Blackwater National Wildlife Refuge, 2145 Key Wallace Dr., Cambridge
410-228-2677, friendsofblackwater.org

Blackwater Adventures, 2524 Key Wallace Dr., Cambridge
410-901-9255, blackwateradventuresmd.com

TIP

Birds aren't the only critters who love Blackwater Refuge. Bring bug spray, and plenty of it.

GO PROGGING
ON SMITH ISLAND

The remote outpost of Smith Island, twelve miles offshore from Crisfield, is almost as hard to get today as it was when it was settled four hundred years ago: boat is your only option. But it's well worth the effort for endless marsh vistas, shy-but-friendly residents (279 at last census), and its lost-in-time vibe. The once-solid landmass is today a series of separate isles, losing ground each year to the encroaching Bay waters. Within the three towns (Ewell, Tylerton and Rhodes Point) you'll find a modest museum, a couple of small shops that may or may not be open, and a few restaurants that typically close by four o'clock. Which means you'll have plenty of time for the lost art of progging—basically, meandering along the shrinking shoreline to see what the tides may have uncovered. (The word descends from British slang for *plundering*—very appropriate for an island settled by British sailors in the 1600s.) The bounty can be anything from shells and sea glass to nineteenth-century pottery shards or ancient arrowheads. But as with all of Smith Island, whatever you find or don't find, the reward is just being there.

visitsmithisland.com

TIP

Smith Island is a dry island—no alcohol is sold anywhere on the island. If you're coming to stay for a few nights, you can bring your own alcohol, but please keep it koozie-covered and drink it in private.

HORSE AROUND
AT ASSATEAGUE

Assateague Island National Seashore is one of the country's most magical places, a protected barrier island with windswept dunes, an inland estuary, and thirty-seven miles of white-sand beach, most of it only accessible by foot. But what makes it most special are its permanent residents: a group of 150 or so wild horses, thought to be descendants of steeds brought by settlers in the late seventeenth century. Chances are you'll spy a band as you drive over the bridge from the mainland, but if not, keep an eye out; they could be out wandering the shoreline or grazing in marsh meadows. Hit up Assateague Outfitters for rental kayaks, canoes, and stand-up paddleboards, ideal for exploring the protected bayside waters. Or bring bikes and pedal the flat, four-mile path along Bayside Drive, stopping for horse sightings on the way. The Atlantic side is great for swimming and surfing the low swells—and yes, horses hit the surf, too.

7206 National Seashore Ln., Berlin
410-641-1441
nps.gov/asis

TIP

Assateague offers drive-in campgrounds, but for the most magical experience, book a beachfront walk-in site on the secluded southern end of the park. Be sure to lock up your food in a sturdy, odor-proof cooler. Rogue horses raid camps scrounging for snacks, which is bad for humans and horses alike.

DROP A LINE
AT BILL BURTON FISHING PIER

If you're hankering to catch some striped bass (or as we call them, rockfish), perch, or trout, bring your rods and bait to Bill Burton Fishing Pier State Park. Even if you're not an angler, it's worth taking the time to stop and stroll this lovely pier, which extends into both sides of the Choptank River, from Talbot County on the west and Dorchester on the east. The pier is what remains of the old US 50 bridge, which was due to be demolished in 1985 when a new, higher bridge was put in place. Fortunately, it was spared in a local campaign spearheaded by *Evening Sun* columnist and avid angler Bill Burton. Now the twenty-five-acre site, with grassy parks on each side, is the perfect place to while away a day. The park is lighted and open around the clock, making it a popular crabbing spot as well.

29761 Bolingbroke Point Dr., Trappe
410-221-2290
dnr.maryland.gov

WATCH THE WEIGH-INS
AT THE WHITE MARLIN OPEN

When it comes to billfish tournaments, things don't get bigger than the White Marlin Open, held every August in Ocean City. The unique topography of offshore deep-water canyons draws mega-size migrating billfish to the region every summer. During the week-long competition, a fleet of anglers head out in the pre-dawn hours to drop their lines, then return in late afternoon with the best of the day's catch of white and blue marlins, tuna, and mahi. Crowds gather by the thousands each evening at bayside Harbour Island for the official weigh-ins. And with record prize money for anglers, the excitement is palpable; in 2018, the largest white marlin earned a payout of $2.5 million. With so many fishermen in one place, the waterfront bars are packed, especially at Harbour Island and Sunset Marina, where most of the competing boats are docked.

423 14th St., Ocean City
410-289-9229
whitemarlinopen.com

SAIL A SKIPJACK
ON THE EASTERN SHORE

The Chesapeake Bay oyster industry wouldn't have existed without the graceful skipjack. Marked by its low sides, raised bow, and single raked mast, these sailing ships were designed for maximum wind power to drag heavy dredges along the bottom of the bay, scooping up bivalves. In the late 1800s, thousands of skipjacks plied the bay, but only an estimated forty or so remain in existence today, the majority on the Eastern Shore. On Tilghman Island, the circa-1886 *Rebecca T. Ruark* is the oldest working skipjack on the bay, while Cambridge's *Nathan of Dorchester* is a newer but historically accurate skipjack, built in 1994; both offer daily sailings from their respective ports. In Annapolis, the circa-1940 *Wilma Lee* is available for dockside tours and sailings via the Annapolis Maritime Museum.

Rebecca T. Ruark
410-886-2176, skipjack.org

Nathan of Dorchester
410-228-7141, skipjack-nathan.org

Wilma Lee
410-295-0104, amaritime.org

Deal Island IslandFest and Skipjack Race
410-784-2785, dealislandchancelionsclub.org

● ●

TIP

Watch the boats in action at two Skipjack Festivals, held every September at Deal Island and Cambridge. Deal Island is the older of the regattas, begun in 1960, and is home to the circa-1906 *Ida May*, reigning champion two years running in 2017 and 2018.

BEHOLD THE SLAUGHTER
ACROSS THE WATER

Set on a peninsula across from downtown Annapolis, the historic watermen's enclave of Eastport has a quirky personality all its own. In 1997, the city of Annapolis temporarily closed the connecting Spa Creek Bridge for repairs, to the dismay of Eastporters, who now had to drive the long way around to get into town. In cheeky retaliation, some residents formed the Maritime Republic of Eastport and officially seceded from the United States. The bridge was soon reopened, but the MRE still flies its yellow flag, and the war is replayed every fall at the Eastport-Annapolis Tug of War. Teams on each side strain to pull a seventeen-hundred-foot rope stretched across Spa Creek while spirited crowds chant "Heave ho!" and "Up the Republic!" The side with the most wins in a series of bouts gets bragging rights for the year. It's a great excuse for a street party, with the revelry going on long after the tugging ends. Eastport usually throws the best bash, with beer trucks, live bands, and the lion's share of rowdy spectators. But in 2018 Annapolis upped their game with a full stage, tented VIP area, and tony food and spirits sponsors. It's a win-win for attendees, who roam from party to party all day long, making the rivalry the ultimate unifier.

Eastport-Annapolis Tug of War
themre.org/tug-of-war

TIP

Not into tugging? Mid-May brings
the MRE's annual .05K Bridge Run, aka
the "least challenging athletic event ever
conceived," where avid and not-so-avid runners
test their endurance with a non-grueling,
barely-five-minute race over the drawbridge
connecting Annapolis to Eastport. The
race is followed by afternoon festivities at
Boatyard Bar & Grill.

CULTURE AND HISTORY

WALK FOUR CENTURIES IN TWO HOURS
WITH WATERMARK TOURS

The city of Annapolis was founded in 1649, which means there's a lot of history along these brick-paved streets and alleyways. Unlike the open-air museum that is Colonial Williamsburg, Annapolis remains a thriving city today—one that happens to have the largest intact collection of revolutionary-era buildings in the country. You'll get a good overview on the entertaining Four Centuries Walking Tour. A colonial-costumed guide takes you inside the state capitol, where George Washington resigned his military commission in 1783; down narrow streets edged by eighteenth-century Georgian mansions and nineteenth-century wooden townhomes; and onto the grounds of the U.S. Naval Academy via the same gate Abraham Lincoln used during the Civil War. Guides put their own slant on history, adding in anything from the boisterous, revolutionary-era Tuesday Night Club to St. John's "Liberty tree" to the tale of the doomed craftsman said to haunt the State House dome.

Annapolis Tours by Watermark
410-268-7601
annapolistours.com

TIP

If you can, book a tour led by the official (really!) town crier, Squire Frederick Taylor. He's a genial font of information, and the tour feels like walking with a celebrity, as people stop and say hi and bus drivers pull over to ask him to give a town cry. You can also book the Squire for private occasions, such as wedding ceremonies.

MARK
THE MASON-DIXON LINE

Back in 1763, Charles Mason and Jeremiah Dixon were hired to help settle a dispute between the Calvert and Penn families over conflicting land charters between the colonial states of Maryland, Pennsylvania, and Delaware. They traveled the country for the next four years, measuring and marking the border with stones. Most of the stones have been lost to time and development, but one of the southernmost markers still stands near Mardela Springs. Located on an unassuming roadside pullout off rural Highway 54, an iron-gated gazebo protects the stones from hands or theft. There are actually three markers here: two smaller ones placed by field scouts, and a 3.5-foot-high crownstone, made of English limestone and engraved on opposite sides with the Calvert and Penn coats of arms. A sign invites you to toss a coin and try to land it atop the largest marker (harder than it sounds, evidenced by the pile of coins just out of arm's reach). Or do as I did and just amuse yourself by stepping back and forth across the unofficial border between North and South.

Transpeninsular Line Midpoint Marker
Rt. 54 near Mardela Springs
visitmaryland.org

CATCH A CROQUET CULTURE CLASH
AT THE ANNAPOLIS CUP

Annapolis is home to two colleges that couldn't be more different: the U.S. Naval Academy, training future military leaders since 1845, and St. John's College, teaching a Great Books curriculum since 1784. The disparate student bodies don't typically interact, except for a single Saturday every April when they cross mallets on the croquet lawn. An offhand challenge from a St. John's College freshman to the USNA commandant back in 1982 led to the annual matchup, called the Annapolis Cup. Each team brings twelve players, who use mallets to advance the ball through a nine-wicket course. The first team to score fourteen points wins. It's easy to tell which team is which; the Middies always match in classic white, while the free-spirited Johnnies switch it up every year, donning anything from Viking helmets to kilts. The community comes out to cheer both sides, donning Gatsby-era duds and turning the day into an ebullient lawn party, supported by champagne and beer trucks, BYO picnics, and live music. The game sells out, so get your tickets in advance; proceeds benefit local charities.

60 College Ave.
410-263-2371
sjc.edu

MEET
THE DELMARVA OTTERS

The Delmarva Discovery Center & Museum is a sixteen-thousand-square-foot gem located in the tiny town of Pocomoke. Hands-on exhibits showcase diverse aspects of regional life, from a Native American canoe on loan from a local tribe to a replica steamship detailing life and routes in a pre-railroad world. Kids can try their hands at oyster tonging or faux-sailing (a fan provides the wind for a twelve-foot catboat) and reach into a touch pool that houses whelks and horseshoe crabs. Other animal exhibits include colorful corn snakes, tiny tree frogs, and a resident diamondback terrapin. But the celebrity attractions are two rescued otters, Mac and Tuck, who swim, slide, and show off in a six-thousand-square-foot, land-and-aquarium habitat. After you visit the museum, test your newfound wildlife-tracking skills on the adjacent 1.25-mile Cypress Park Nature Trail, which runs along the river.

Delmarva Discovery Center & Museum
2 Market St., Pocomoke City
410-957-9933, delmarvadiscoverycenter.org

TIP
Time your visit for the noontime feeding, when you'll find Mac and Tuck at their most attentive and playful.

CHEER ON A CRAB
IN CRISFIELD

The National Hard Crab Derby is an only-in-Maryland tradition, held every Labor Day weekend in Crisfield. When it began in 1947, races took place on the street in front of the post office. These days, the hard-shelled contenders make tracks down a purpose-built race track—basically a slick, fast board. The track is set up on an angle, which is more conducive to getting the crabs moving (evidently not all of them know they're racing) and for spectators to follow their favorite crustaceans as they sidle through a series of heats until there's one crab left standing. Along with the races, don't miss the crab-picking contest, where veteran crab processors—many of whom work in nearby seafood plants—compete to see who can pick the most meat in a fifteen-minute period. The Miss Crustacean beauty pageant, a crab-cooking contest, a 10K run, and a high-stakes boat-docking contest round out the weekend's events.

Downtown Crisfield
410-968-2500
nationalhardcrabderby.com

DISCOVER THE DECOYS
AT THE WARD MUSEUM
OF WILDFOWL ART

The use of wildfowl decoys for hunting can be traced back to Native Americans, who used deceptively carved stand-ins to lure wildfowl into close range before the days of rifles. But it was siblings Lem and Samuel Ward who elevated the genre to art with their delicately realistic wooden carvings of ducks, geese, and more, done out of a humble studio in Crisfield from the 1920s through the 1950s. Their work earned them accolades from *National Geographic* to the National Endowments for the Arts, plus avid collectors around the world. You'll marvel at the detail on the pieces showcased at the Ward Museum of Wildfowl Art, home to the largest public collection of decorative decoys in the world. It's fascinating to see the changing styles of craftsmanship over one hundred years of work from carvers around the country, not to mention the differing beauty of the species showcased, from natty pintails to snow geese midflight.

909 S. Schumaker Dr., Salisbury
410-742-4988
wardmuseum.org

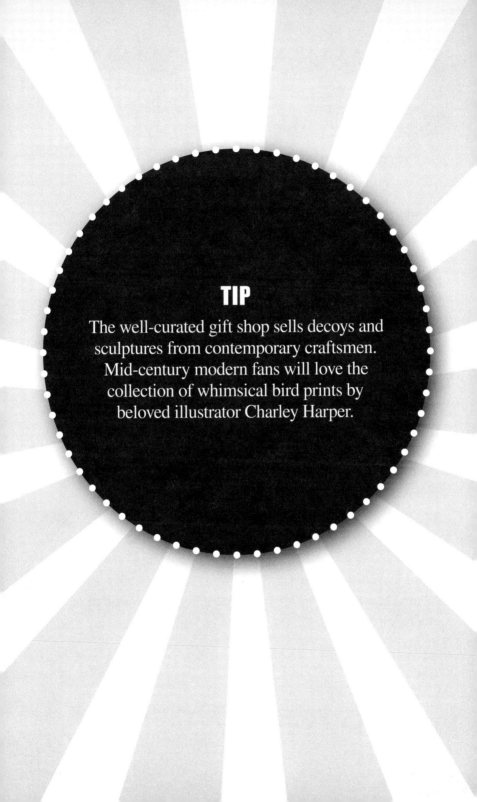

TIP

The well-curated gift shop sells decoys and sculptures from contemporary craftsmen. Mid-century modern fans will love the collection of whimsical bird prints by beloved illustrator Charley Harper.

WATCH
PRESERVATION IN PROGRESS

In 2016, Historic Annapolis undertook a multi-year restoration of the circa-1767 James Brice House, the largest Georgian mansion in downtown Annapolis. This offers a unique opportunity for history buffs: the chance to don a hard hat and go behind the scaffolding to witness the work in progress. Depending on the day, the reservation-only tour may have you going over finds from cultural archaeologists, watching stone masons shore up the English ballast-brick walls, or catching artisans doing painstaking recovery of centuries-old plasterwork.

For post-restoration tours, the stately William Paca House has two floors of finished rooms plus a formal terraced garden, as it would have looked when the signer of the Declaration of Independence lived there. The circa-1773 Hammond-Harwood House features gorgeous woodwork, rare furnishings by cabinetmaker John Shaw, and portraits by Charles Willson Peale. The modest, wood-frame Hogshead recreates the home life of the lower-class tradespeople who would have rented this humble dwelling back in the 1800s. Historic Annapolis offers creative events throughout the year, from themed happy hours to sell-out garden parties, designed to let the community interact with the homes in a less structured way than a traditional museum visit.

James Brice House
42 East St.

William Paca House & Garden
186 Prince George St.

Hogshead
43 Pinkney St.

Hammond-Harwood House Museum
19 Maryland Ave., 410-263-4683
hammondharwoodhouse.org

Historic Annapolis
410-267-7619, annapolis.org

RIDE THE NATION'S OLDEST PRIVATE FERRY
IN OXFORD

The channel separating the towns of Oxford and Bellevue is less than a mile wide, but if you can't cross it, you'll need to drive thirty miles around the headwater of the Tred Avon River to get to the other side. Enter the Oxford-Bellevue ferry, which began operation in 1683 and, under the proprietorship of Tom and Judy Bixler, remains the oldest privately owned ferry route in the country. Walk or drive onboard at the Oxford landing, and about ten minutes later, you'll dock in even tinier Bellevue. You can disembark or take the ride back to Oxford; the boat runs on a continuous circuit every fifteen to twenty minutes. Your destination doesn't really matter. It's the journey that counts, especially if you're lucky enough to catch the last ferry of the day, just before sunset, when the golden light reflects off the water and the ospreys are returning home after their final fishing trips of the day. It's pure magic, wherever you're headed.

101 E. Strand, Oxford
410-745-9023, oxfordferry.com

TIP
Like the best things in life, this one is limited, with service running daily from mid-April through October, and on weekends only in November.

HEED THE CALL OF THE NOT-SO-ANCIENT MARINER
AT CHESAPEAKE BAY MARITIME MUSEUM

Chesapeake Bay Maritime Museum offers so much that museum seems too small a word. Set waterfront in St. Michaels, this eighteen-acre complex is a treasure trove of maritime life, past and present. Exhibits in multiple buildings showcase life on the Bay, from vintage pleasure boats in the At Play on the Bay exhibit to a full warehouse replicating the oyster industry from boat to table. Climb up the winding staircase of the renovated lighthouse to hear stories of how keepers managed their tasks in the 1800s, then head out on the water on the fleet of boats—including 1920s buyboat *Winnie Estelle* and the 1889 *Edna E. Lockwood*, the oldest log-bottom bugeye still sailing. The Apprentice for a Day program encourages you join the staff in hands-on learning, from reading navigational charts to bronze casting. Any time of year, you're invited to watch shipwrights ply their skills in the museum's working shipyard, be it crafting a log canoe sailboat from scratch or their current project, building a new, historically accurate recreation of *Maryland Dove*, the 17th-century ship that first brought settlers to the Chesapeake in 1634.

213 N. Talbot St., St. Michaels
410-745-2916, cbmm.org

PLAY MIDDIE FOR ME
AT U.S. NAVAL ACADEMY

Established in 1845, the U.S. Naval Academy has a symbiotic relationship with Annapolis. You'll see uniformed midshipmen (the term denotes military rank, and thus applies to both men and women) all over town, and Main Street is lined with shops selling Navy sweatshirts and stuffed versions of mascot Bill the Goat. But you're missing out if you don't visit the campus itself. Start at the Armel-Leftwich Visitor Center for an overview of Academy student life. Bancroft Hall will wow you with its sheer size: with 4.8 miles of corridors, it's the largest single dormitory in the United States and the mothership for the school's 4,400 students. The domed USNA Chapel is a must, both for the Tiffany stained-glass windows and the below-ground crypt of the "Father of the Navy," John Paul Jones. Time your visit to catch Noon Formation, when the full Brigade of Midshipmen gathers in formation outside Bancroft Hall for presentation of the colors before heading in to their midday meal.

Armel-Leftwich Visitor Center, 52 King St.
410-293-8687
usna.edu

TIP

The USNA is a government site and, as such, security is tight. Visitors park in Annapolis and enter on foot via Gate One, at the foot of Prince George Street. You'll need to show a government-issued ID such as a driver's license, passport, or REAL ID in order to enter.

MEET AN ENGINEERING MARVEL
ON THE C&D CANAL

The brainstorm of Dutch settler and cartographer Augustine Herman back in the 1600s, the Chesapeake & Delaware (C&D) Canal was dug by hand in 1824 in a farsighted effort to cut short the three-hundred-mile ocean trip between Philadelphia and Baltimore. The series of locks on the waterway remained active through the 1930s, when the canal was dredged deep enough to make the locks unnecessary. Today, the still-active shipping channel is a picturesque way-through for ships, edged by Chesapeake City's quaint blocks of Victorian-era homes turned into shops, restaurants, and B&Bs. Start your visit at the self-guided C&D Canal Museum, where the original steam-powered lifting wheel is on display in the stone pumphouse. Then stroll along the water's edge via the eighteen-mile Ben Cardin C&D Canal Trail, gazing in awe at the towering tankers and cruise ships that pass through what is still one of the busiest canals in the world. The juxtaposition of rural Victorian and modern megaship superhighway is fascinating.

85 Bethel Rd., Chesapeake City
410-885-5622
chesapeakecity.com

DISCOVER THE NAVY'S BEST-KEPT SECRET
AT U.S. NAVAL ACADEMY MUSEUM

Located in unassuming Preble Hall, the U.S. Naval Academy Museum is often overlooked for the more scenic parts of the Academy, but it holds a treasure trove of naval history. First-floor exhibits span the history of the Navy, from the Revolutionary War to the present, highlighting alumni participation in everything from space exploration to Nobel prizes. On the second deck is a wide assortment of paintings and prints, spanning key military battles to WWI Liberty Bond lithographs. Even more intriguing is the display of seventeenth- and eighteenth-century ship models, the largest collection in the country, representing with exquisite detail almost every type of war ship from the 1600s. You can't help but be moved by the models made by French POWs from the bones of their beef rations during the Napoleonic wars—powerful stuff indeed.

118 Maryland Ave.
410-293-2108
unsa.edu/Museum

VISIT THE ROOM
WHERE IT HAPPENED

Psst, Lin-Manuel Miranda . . . arguably, the *real* room where it happened is at the Maryland State House in Annapolis. Dating back to 1772 (though not finished until 1797 due to the war), it's the oldest continuously operating state house in the country. A statue of George Washington in the Old Senate Chamber marks the exact spot where he resigned as Commander in Chief of the Continental Army in 1783, thus ensuring that the United States remained a democracy following the Revolutionary War. And the surrounding rooms are where it still happens, as the State House remains the seat of government for the Maryland General Assembly. Other must-sees inside include a Charles Willson Peale painting of Washington, Lafayette, and Tilghman; portraits of Maryland's four signers of the Declaration of Independence; and a copy of Washington's resignation speech, displayed under glass. The domed roof, which is the highest point in Annapolis, is the largest wooden dome constructed without nails in the country, capped off with a lightning rod designed by Benjamin Franklin.

The Maryland State House, 100 State Circle
410-946-5000
visitmaryland.org/listing/groups/maryland-state-house

TIP

The State House is open to visitors every day of the year except Christmas and New Year's Day. Self-guided tour information is available onsite, or sign up for a more involved visit with Watermark Tours. Photo IDs are required for entrance, as is a metal detector scan.

BURN YOUR SOCKS
IN EASTPORT

Back in the 1970s, an Eastport resident decided to welcome the vernal equinox (and unofficial start of boating season) by burning the socks he'd worn all winter. He invited a few friends to join him, and thus a uniquely Annapolis tradition was born. The now-annual sock burning has added a few more elements since then: the reciting of "Ode to the Equinox," an oyster-shucking contest, the People's Choice competition for best oyster dish from local restaurants (Blackwall Hitch took the prize in 2019), and live music by the Eastport Oyster Boys, whose Bay-themed songs are a required soundtrack at Eastport's most important events. (See *Behold The Slaughter Across The Water*.) The event is held on the lawn at the Annapolis Maritime Museum, and proceeds go to support the museum's educational outreach.

723 Second St.
410-295-0104
amaritime.org

NOTE
"Ode to the Equinox" has been updated over the years, and is always fitting for the occasion. But my favorite is the original, from 1994, which encapsulates the spirit of Eastport.

ODE TO THE EQUINOX

By Jefferson Holland, Poet Laureate of Eastport, 1994

Them Eastport boys got an odd tradition
When the sun swings to its equinoxical position,
They build a little fire down along the docks,
They doff their shoes and they burn their winter socks.

Yes, they burn their socks at the equinox
You might think that's peculiar, but I think it's not,
See, they're the same socks they put on last fall,
And they never took 'em off to wash 'em, not at all

So they burn their socks at the equinox
In a little ol' fire burnin' nice and hot,
Some think incineration is the only solution,
'Cause washin' 'em contributes to the Chesapeake's pollution

Through the spring and the summer and into the fall,
They go around not wearin' any socks at all,
Just stinky bare feet stuck in old deck shoes
Whether out on the water or enjoyin' a brew

So if you sail into the harbor on the 20th of March
And smell a smell like limburger mixed in with laundry starch,
You'll know you're downwind of the Eastport docks
Where they're burning their socks for the equinox.

CLIMB A LIGHTHOUSE
AT THOMAS POINT SHOAL

If anything rivals the Bay Bridge as an icon of the region, it would be the Thomas Point Shoal Lighthouse. This white, hexagonal-cottage lighthouse has guarded a shoal at the mouth of the South River since 1875, and it's the only screw-pile lighthouse on the Bay that's still in its original location. You can spy it from afar at Thomas Point Park in Annapolis, but to really get to know it, sign up for a tour, done in conjunction with the U.S. Lighthouse Society and the Annapolis Maritime Museum. The thirty-minute boat ride takes you from museum dock to the lighthouse, giving great photo ops as you approach. Once moored, a docent takes you up a steel ladder and inside the structure for an hour-long tour, detailing everything from a keeper's work and lifestyle to the lighting mechanics that allow it to shine at a distance over ten miles. Tours are only offered on select Saturdays and capped at eighteen people. They usually sell out, so book early.

723 Second St.
410-295-0104
amaritime.org

TIP

Set in a former oyster-packing plant overlooking the water in Eastport, the much-loved Annapolis Maritime Museum celebrates the Bay's heritage via in-house exhibits, expert-helmed lectures, and hands-on school programs, giving it a community impact much larger than its physical footprint.

LEARN THE LEGACY
OF KUNTA KINTE

Alex Haley's epic novel, *Roots: The Saga of an American Family,* became a worldwide phenomenon in the 1970s, telling the story of Haley's ancestors, who first came to this country as slaves in the eighteenth century. What's the Annapolis connection? When Haley's great-great-great-grandfather Kunta Kinte was kidnapped from Africa, it was here that the slave ship cleared customs and Kunta Kinte was sold at auction. Today, a three-part memorial pays tribute to Haley's ancestor and all of those forced into slavery. On City Dock, life-size bronze statues depict the author reading to children. Just adjacent, along Compromise Street, ten plaques share different passages from the book. Across the street is a granite-and-bronze compass dial with a map of the world and Annapolis at its center. Together with a depiction of ship conditions and a slave auction listing from a 1767 issue of the *Maryland Gazette*, the memorial provides a powerful glimpse into this horrifying era of American history and acts as a testament to the power of the human spirit.

240-801-5543, kuntakinte.org

TIP
Every September, City Dock comes alive with music, dancing, and spoken word at the Kunta Kinte Heritage Festival, which celebrates thirty years in 2019.

TOSS YOUR TEA
AT THE CHESTERTOWN
TEA PARTY FESTIVAL

The Boston Tea Party gets all the ink in the history books, but it wasn't the only protest of its kind. When the good citizens of Chestertown learned that the British had closed the port of Boston, they responded in kind, passing a resolution that banned the importing, selling, or consuming of tea, and tossing their own chests of tea into the Chesapeake. Ok, so some historians dispute that last part . . . but Chestertown celebrates the legend with a weekend-long party held every May. There's a tea-tossing reenactment, naturally, and a colonial-style parade. But the highlight is the Raft Race, where competitors create their own floating designs out of non-nautical materials and attempt to race their way around a course before they sink. (Spoiler alert: Not all of them make it.) Add in street vendors and Maryland wine and craft beer tastings, and you have one of the best parties on the Shore.

Downtown Chestertown
410-778-1361
chestertownteaparty.org

VISIT
LONDON [TOWN]

Located on the South River, Historic London Town was settled in the 1600s as a ferry stop on the route from Annapolis to parts north (consider it the Route 50 of its day). Unlike the revolutionary-era millionaire mansions you'll find in Annapolis, this open-air museum was once a working-class town, populated by carpenters, ironsmiths, and traders. As the Executive Director Rod Cofield says, "Unless you're a billionaire, this is the kind of town you would have lived in British America." The centerpiece is the stately red-brick William Brown House, built as a tavern in 1700s and displayed as it would have been used then. Recent restorations have added a wood-plank tenement house and carpenter's shop, built to colonial-era design specifications. Costumed reenactors and craftspeople bring the place to life during the year, especially at their signature event, Immersion Day, held every October.

839 Londontown Rd., Edgewater
410-222-1919, historiclondontown.org

TIP
Nature lovers will enjoy the eight acres of trail-laced woodland gardens. A loyal band of volunteer gardeners keeps them beautiful, and it's fascinating to watch the foliage change throughout the seasons.

GET TO KNOW
FREDERICK DOUGLASS

Abolitionist leader Frederick Douglass was born into slavery in Talbot County before escaping at age twenty and heading north, where he became the most prominent orator-author of his day. Maryland has multiple sites devoted to him, including some on the Eastern Shore. Opened in 2018 on the two-hundredth anniversary of his birth, Frederick Douglass Park on the Tuckahoe seeks to capture the landscape of his childhood, which he so vividly recalled in his books. A life-size sculpture at Talbot County Courthouse in Easton marks where he gave his groundbreaking "Self-Made Men" speech in 1859. He built his retirement home in the African American summer community of Highland Beach, outside Annapolis; though he never actually lived there, it's now a small museum, open by appointment. Learn more about him and the greater context of African American culture at the small but robust Banneker-Douglass Museum, located in an 1874 brick church in downtown Annapolis.

Frederick Douglass Park on the Tuckahoe
13211 Lewiston Rd., Queen Anne
410-770-8050

Banneker-Douglass Museum
84 Franklin St.
410-216-6180
bdmuseum.maryland.gov

SEE THE BLUE ANGELS
ON THE SEVERN RIVER

Annapolitans have conflicting emotions about Commissioning Week. The annual graduation ceremony at the U.S. Naval Academy brings tens of thousands of people to town to see their loved ones graduate, which means traffic jams, clueless pedestrians crossing streets, road closures depending on the commencement speaker, and the inability to get a reservation at any restaurant within walking distance of downtown. But it also brings out a sense of patriotism and the chance to see the Blue Angels, the Navy's high-flying performance team. The team of six F/A-18 Hornets performs every year on the Wednesday before Commencement, thrilling viewers with their daredevil rolls, loops, and precise formations, sometimes flying hundreds of miles per hour at just eighteen inches apart. The show takes place above the Severn River, and thousands of boaters take to the water to enjoy the performance, adding to the spectacle. Great viewing spots include Ingram Field and Hospital Point on the Academy; Jonas Green Park, under the Severn River Bridge; and Spa Creek Bridge in Annapolis. If you want to watch from the water, Watermark Cruises offers a series of cruises that take you close to the action.

visitannapolis.org/events/annual/commissioning-week

Watermark Cruises
410-268-7601
cruisesonthebay.org

TIP

The Blue Angels always do a practice session the afternoon before the big show, which is a great chance to see them sans crowds. On Commencement Day itself, they perform a low pass over Navy–Marine Corps Memorial Stadium as a congratulatory nod to the graduating class.

CELEBRATE WATERFOWL IN EVERY FORM
AT THE WATERFOWL FESTIVAL

Every November, art patrons, camo-clad hunting enthusiasts, and world-renowned duck callers head to downtown Easton for this unique, weekend-long sportsman's-expo-meets-art-festival. The downtown streets are closed to accommodate the crowds, who wander in and out of the galleries along Harrison and Dover streets, checking out juried selections of nature-inspired pieces from around the country. Bands perform on a street-corner stage, keeping the energy up, while vendors serve hot cider and cups of cream of crab soup to keep revelers warm. Across town at Easton High School, skilled participants from around the globe vie for the title of best goose or duck caller at the World Waterfowl Calling Championships. You can also watch Chesapeake Bay retrievers show off their moves at the Bay Street Ponds, or sample Maryland-made adult beverages at the all-day tasting pavilion.

40 S. Harrison St., Easton
410-822-4567
waterfowlfestival.org

FOLLOW HARRIET TUBMAN
AT THE UNDERGROUND RAILROAD NATIONAL HISTORICAL PARK

Underground Railroad pioneer Harriet Tubman was born into slavery in 1822 in Dorchester County, and much of her rescue work took place in the extensive network of tobacco plantations on the antebellum Eastern Shore. Start off at the state-of-the-art visitor center, where multimedia exhibits shed light on her daring escape and multiple return visits to free family and friends, along with a greater context of the realities of slave life and the work of supportive abolitionists along the Underground Railroad. Then get in your car and head out on the Harriet Tubman Byway, which winds for 125 miles through the countryside. There are thirty-six stopping points along the way, including the site of the Brodess farm, where she was born; the still-intact Bucktown Village Store, where Tubman was injured when she tried to protect a slave from his enraged master; and Choptank Landing, near where she made her first escape.

4068 Golden Hill Rd., Church Creek
410-221-2290
nps.gov/hatu

410-228-1000
harriettubmanbyway.org

GO FULL TUDOR
AT MARYLAND RENAISSANCE FESTIVAL

Situated in a rural suburb of Annapolis, the Tudor village of Revel Grove stands dormant most of the year but comes to life every fall with the Maryland Renaissance Festival. An estimated three hundred fifty thousand merrymakers descend over nine weekends to enjoy jousters, fire-eaters, jesters, and more at one of the nation's oldest Renaissance fairs. There is literally something for everyone: twelve stages keep up a packed slate of performances from juggling shows to Shakespeare (think *"Macbeth* in 20 Minutes or Less"), while strolling performers do sleight of hand or period ballads. Don't miss the jousters, who face off on horseback in the packed arena. Audience participation is at the heart of RennFest, and attendees oblige, sporting corsets, kilts, capes, and more. Don't own period duds? An onsite booth rents costumes for daily use, while a slew of vendors sells everything from mystic-inspired jewelry to leather tunics that would fit right in on *Game of Thrones*.

1821 Crownsville Rd.
800-296-7304
rennfest.com

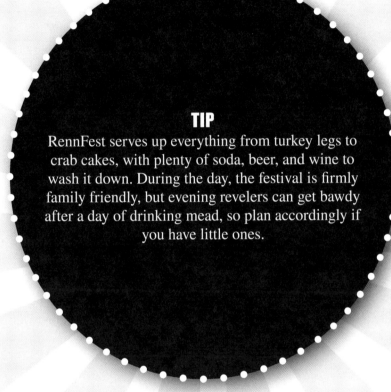

TIP

RennFest serves up everything from turkey legs to crab cakes, with plenty of soda, beer, and wine to wash it down. During the day, the festival is firmly family friendly, but evening revelers can get bawdy after a day of drinking mead, so plan accordingly if you have little ones.

HOUSE CRASH AFTER HOURS
AT ANNAPOLIS BY CANDLELIGHT

Most of the historic buildings in downtown Annapolis are privately owned, which means the only way you can get inside is by invitation from the owner. But once a year, in early November, Historic Annapolis presents Annapolis by Candlelight. In this self-paced, evening walking tour, ticketed strollers head to one of Annapolis's oldest neighborhoods, armed with a map marking the addresses of fifteen or so open houses. Docents at each residence shed light on the unique history and architecture, as well as the renovations made to turn these centuries-old buildings into gorgeous, twenty-first–century homes. Call it part voyeurism, part history lesson, and part interior design class, but it's always a big success, drawing more than twenty-five hundred participants while raising money for Historic Annapolis.

410-267-7619
annapolis.org/historic/events

GET YOUR MOTOR RUNNING
IN ST. MICHAELS

You never know what you'll find at the Classic Motor Museum in St. Michaels. Though it's only been open since August 2017, it's already the go-to for gearheads and antique lovers in the Mid-Atlantic. The small but impressive permanent collection includes a 1936 Ford Phaeton and a 1932 Ford Model B. Collectors around the region are so excited about the venture, they're opening their own garages and lending rarities to be displayed in the warehouse. Recent displays included a 1938 Bugatti Stelvio (which at auction can cost nearly one million dollars) and a more attainable but perfectly pristine 1967 Camaro. Equally impressive is their onsite student chapter of the Antique Automobile Club of America, which gives local teenagers the chance to learn the art of restoring vintage autos. It's a fitting addition to a town that hosts the prestigious Concours d'Elegance every September.

102 E. Marengo St., St. Michaels
410-745-8979
classicmotormuseum.org

OVERNIGHT
IN TWO OF AMERICA'S OLDEST INNS

Maryland Inn, located in Annapolis, opened its doors in 1727 and has been operating as a hotel ever since. Members of the Continental Congress stayed here, and George Washington danced at parties in the second-floor ballroom. Check into room 1417, which is the only one with a water view. Looking down Main Street to the placid harbor, you get a real sense of what the town must have felt like back when it was the fourth-largest port on the Eastern seaboard.

English merchant Robert Morris settled in tiny, riverfront Oxford in 1710. His house operated as a tavern, general store, and World War II convalescent home before becoming a full-time inn in the 1940s. The Heritage Colonial rooms are original to the main house, featuring river views and period details like handmade wood-paneled walls and fireplaces made from seventeenth-century English ballast brick. Dinner in front of the fireplace at cozy Salter's Tavern is a must, and the acclaimed chef offers cooking classes and themed wine dinners throughout the year. Over its long life, the Robert Morris Inn has hosted celebs including Walter Cronkite and Elizabeth Taylor, and James Michener outlined his novel *Chesapeake* here in the 1970s.

Maryland Inn, 16 Church Circle
410-263-2641, historicinnsofannapolis.com

Robert Morris Inn, 314 N. Morris St., Oxford
410-226-5111, robertmorrisinn.com

CELEBRATE THE SEASON
AT THE LIGHTS PARADE

Every December, a one-night-only transformation takes over Annapolis Harbor. As the winter sky darkens, boats gather silently in Spa Creek, lining up to make their debut. At precisely six o'clock, the signal sounds and all of the boats press the "on" button, transforming the scene into a brilliant spectacle of seasonal lights floating across the water. For the next two hours, the costumed boats parade in and out of Ego Alley, lights flashing and carols blasting, while spectators lined up along City Dock and Spa Creek Bridge marvel at their creativity. And what creativity there is, from tugboats dressed up as Rudolph to optical illusions like a motorboat transformed into the wood-paneled station wagon from *National Lampoon's Christmas Vacation*. A panel of judges chooses the official winners, with prize money to match. But this is really a case where just showing up is reward enough; it's a highlight of the holiday season.

844-INFO-EYC
eastportyc.org/lights-parade

EMBRACE THE ARTS
AT THE MITCHELL GALLERY

Annapolitans either love the Mitchell Gallery or don't know about it yet. This two-room gallery at St. John's College is accredited by the American Alliance of Museums and brings in exhibits that you'd expect to find in a much larger venue. Their four major shows per year have covered artists such as Matisse and Warhol, but also children's book illustrations, sixteenth-century illuminated manuscripts, and renowned printmakers. In addition to touring exhibits, the gallery curates at least one annual show focused on regional artists. Each collection also brings an opportunity to get creative, with a "Try It" workshop: an artist-led, hands-on class related to a skill on display in the show. Held in a classroom at the adjacent Mellon Hall, the classes hold fifteen people max and sell out, so sign up early if you're game.

St. John's College, 60 College Ave.
410-626-2556
sjc.edu/annapolis/mitchell-gallery

TIP

Founded in 1696 as King William's School,
St. John's is the third-oldest college in the
country. With its stately three-hundred-year-
old McDowell Hall and bucolic lawn stretching
down to College Creek, you'd never know it has
a dramatic history as a secret gathering place for
revolution-minded colonists and as a Union
hospital during the Civil War.

SIT AND REFLECT
AT THIRD HAVEN MEETING HOUSE

Colonial America's roots are intertwined with Quakerism. William Penn founded the Pennsylvania colony as a place of equality and religious tolerance, and there were Quakers all over Maryland from its earliest days. Third Haven Meeting House in Easton is a living testament to their history. Tucked in a grove of old-growth trees just off a busy street, you'd never know it was there unless you were looking for it. The white, wood-frame cabin was constructed in 1682, making it the oldest surviving Friends meeting house in the country. An extension added on the western side in 1797 created its unique, off-kilter exterior, and the house is still used for services by the Religious Society of Friends today. The door doesn't have a lock, so visitors can go in whenever they wish. The minimalist interior has rows of plain wooden benches and no ornamentation whatsoever, just natural light filtering in from the side windows, making it a perfect place for quiet contemplation.

405 S. Washington St., Easton
410-822-0293
thirdhaven.org

SAIL A TALL SHIP
IN CHESTERTOWN

In fall 2001, schooner *Sultana* (a 1768 British Navy replica) and *Pride of Baltimore II* (a reproduction nineteenth-century clipper ship) took a sail down the Chester River, marking the end of the sailing season before taking down their rigging for the winter. The crews had so much fun that they decided to repeat the voyage the next year. It has since grown into Downrigging Weekend Tall Ship & Wooden Boat Festival. Every October in Chestertown, *Sultana* and *Pride* are joined by other tall ships, including circa-1900 *Lady Maryland*, skipjack *Elsworth*, and *Kalmar Nyckel,* a recreated Swedish settlement ship. It's rare enough to see a collection of boats like this in one place, but this festival also offers public sails, so you can get out and experience them on the water. The array of privately owned wooden boats is always intriguing; you never know what you'll see, be it a 1920s oyster hauler or a natty 1970s picnic boat. Lectures offer context on maritime history, while food and drink keep the party going in one of best-preserved colonial seaports in the United States.

Chestertown waterfront
410-778-5954
sultanaeducation.org

SHOPPING AND FASHION

BUY A BOAT
(OR JUST PRETEND TO)
AT THE ANNAPOLIS BOAT SHOW

Thinking about buying a boat? Then head to the Annapolis Boat Show, the largest in-water boat show in the country, which takes over downtown Annapolis for two weekends in October. One week is devoted to sailboats, the other to powerboats. Even if you're not in the market for a vessel, it's worth a visit to take in the spectacle. Dealers showcase their latest models along miles of purpose-built floating docks, and most are open for climb-aboard tours. If you're new to cruising, onsite instructors will take you out on the Severn River and teach you the basics, so you'll know how to captain should you get the urge to purchase. And if you don't have the cash, no problem—you can get appraisals and finance loans on the spot. There's no shortage of shore-side shopping, either, with massive tents featuring everything from the latest in galley kitchenware and foul-weather gear to snazzy boat shoes and doggy life jackets.

410-268-8828, annapolisboatshows.com

TIP
Can't make it for the big shebang? There are two smaller shows in April, with sailboats at City Dock and powerboats at the Bay Bridge Boat Show across the water in Stevensville.

TOP IT OFF
AT HATS IN THE BELFRY

Hats are having a moment, but Hats in the Belfry doesn't worry about trends. As they say, "Hats may go in and out of fashion, but there are *always* hat people." In the last forty years, this Annapolis store has grown from a small haberdashery to one of the nation's most respected purveyors of toppers. The flagship on Main Street is where it all began. The sweeping collection spans British trilbys and flapper-style cloches to cowboy hats, woolen fisherman's caps, and feathered hatinators that would fit right in at Ascot. Especially cool is their Handmade for Belfry collection: unique designs made to their specifications by classic brands including Stetson, Biltmore, and Bollman. Don't know a boater from a bowler? Staff will walk you through the need-to-knows. Not a hat person? Be forewarned: Walking in these doors just might just make you one.

103 Main St.
410-268-6333
hatsinthebelfry.com

SUPPORT AN ARTIST
AT A LOCAL GALLERY

There are talented artists all over the Shore, and too many good galleries to list them all. But here's an opinionated start. In Annapolis, Nancy Hammond Editions' paintings and cut-paper work pay colorful homage to boats, herons, waterside flora, and black labs, one of which always makes an appearance in her limited-edition annual posters. Artist Charles Lawrance runs the collective FinArt, which showcases an eclectic variety of nontraditional art and sculpture in a shared studio with gallery/classroom ArtFarm. For photography, the Annapolis Collection Gallery has a standout array of historic prints and contemporary shots of life along the Bay, including signed works by local phenom Jay Fleming.

In Easton, Troika Gallery specializes in classical-technique painting and sculpture, with an emphasis on landscapes and portraiture. In Chestertown, acclaimed curator Carla Massoni showcases world-renowned artists in her airy second-floor gallery, with difficult-to-procure pieces.

Nancy Hammond Editions, 192 West St.
410-295-6612, nancyhammondeditions.com

FinArt Gallery & Studios, 111 Chinquapin Round Rd.
443-254-2787, finartannapolis.com

The Annapolis Collection Gallery, 55 West St.
410-280-1414, annapoliscollection.com

Troika Gallery, 9 S. Harrison St., Easton, 410-770-9190, troikagallery.com

Carla Massoni Gallery, 203 High St., Chestertown
410-778-7330, massoniart.com

TIP

Want to watch artists at work? At Plein Air Easton and Paint Annapolis festivals, juried artists paint al fresco, with curious onlookers taking note of their progress. Each event culminates with a party and sale of works created over the week.

STOCK UP ON SURF WEAR
IN BERLIN

Set in a bright-blue bungalow midway between Ocean City and Assateague Island, Assateague Island Surf Shop brings a taste of California style to the Atlantic Coast. They have everything you need for a week at the beach, and it's a refreshing step up from the typical T-shirts and towels you'll find over on the OC boardwalk— instead, think Birdwell surf trunks, RVCA rompers, reclaimed canvas beach totes, surf-inspired jewelry, and flip flops galore. It's all carefully curated by the owners, a married couple with a keen eye for style and quality. But looking good isn't all that matters here: there are beach bikes for rent and surfboards for rent or purchase. An onsite café sells smoothies, sandwiches, and açaí bowls, so you can fuel up healthfully before hitting the swells.

8315 Stephen Decatur Hwy., Berlin
410-973-2632
assateagueislandsurfshop.com

EXPLORE ECLECTIC SHOPS
ALONG MARYLAND AVENUE

To me, there is no prettier place to window shop than Maryland Avenue. During the eighteenth century, this was the most fashionable street in Annapolis, up the hill from the then-sordid waterfront. Today, the charming, brick-paved street is lined with boutiques selling intriguing wares out of tidy eighteenth- and nineteenth-century storefronts. Natalie Silitch Designs showcases her own whimsical folk art alongside an ever-changing array of antiques, Annabeth's is a corner grocer for necessities (which is what I call wine and gourmet snacks), and Capital Custom Clothiers offers custom-made suits and menswear. Update your vinyl collection at KA-CHUNK!! Records, score a mid-century treasure at Evergreen Antiques & True Vintage, and browse for books at Annapolis Bookstore or Old Fox Books. If you need fortification, grab a Boat Guys Blend (French roast meets mocha java) at City Dock Coffee or something stronger at Galway Bay, a cozy Irish pub.

shopmarylandavenue.com

GET GROWING
AT HOMESTEAD GARDENS

How to describe all that is Homestead Gardens? This garden/décor/whatever-else-you-need store is the largest enclosed garden center in Maryland, drawing landscapers and gardeners (whether practicing or aspiring) from Anne Arundel and South counties and beyond. They have more than three-hundred-thirty-thousand-square feet of growing space, with annuals, perennials, trees, and shrubs in every color and variety you can imagine, plus all the supplies you need to keep your plants happy and healthy at home. Not a gardener? You'll also find chic outdoor furniture, a huge assortment of grills, women's apparel and accessories, and even something for Fido or Mittens. (Bring Fido along; the whole place is dog friendly.) Their hands-on staff and full slate of gardening classes help turn even the blackest of thumbs green.

743 W. Central Ave., Davidsonville
410-798-5000, homesteadgardens.com

OUTBID THE PROS
AT DIXON'S FURNITURE AUCTION

Ever wonder how antique stores get their hands on such cool finds? Chances are they've hit up Dixon's Furniture Auction in Crumpton, which has been held in an unassuming rural warehouse for more than fifty years. Vendors arrive at dawn to set up their lots inside or out on the lawn, with items loosely grouped into categories: furniture, tabletop, jewelry, and household wares. Bidders arrive early to stroll the lots, poker faces intact lest their excitement alert a competing bidder to something of interest. At nine o'clock, the live auctioneer starts his rounds, moving via cart from lot to lot, trailed by attentive buyers giving a nod or lifting a number to place a bid. You never know what you might find: seventeenth-century side chairs, mid-century floor lamps, stately French armoires, elegant estate jewelry and tchotchkes galore (I scored a 1950s wicker elephant stand for sixty dollars!)—and that's what keeps it so interesting.

2017 Dudley Corners Rd., Crumpton
410-928-3006, crumptonauctions.com

TIP
Impulse buying is a danger at auctions. To help, Dixon's requires you to pre-set a spending limit when you get your bidder number. But you can always go back and add more if something pricier catches your eye.

COZY UP WITH A BOOK
AT A COOL INDIE BOOKSTORE

Independent bookstores are having a revival as people seek a real connection with what they read and their communities at large. The best bookstores offer a welcoming staff, a well-curated selection of books, and a varied slate of events that get people talking—and these have that in spades. The best ones in our region offer both new and gently used tomes, and have special sections dedicated to area interest, from regional history and nature books detailing the Bay's ecosystem to titles from local authors. Don't see what you're looking for? Just ask. A great bookseller will always help you hunt down titles, and do special orders. Think of these standouts as your own personal Amazon, but so much better.

TIP
If comics and graphic novels are more your thing, make a beeline to Third Eye Comics, which stocks the latest releases, along with games and collectibles, and hosts an array of writer and artist signings.
209 Chinquapin Round Rd.
410-897-0322

OLD FOX BOOKS & COFFEESHOP,

The book and gift selection is personal and ever-changing at this neighborhood charmer on Maryland Avenue, which blends historic brick with cozy armchairs, oriental rugs, a fireplace, and communal tables ideal for any of their four book clubs. A spiral staircase leads to a trove of used books in the stone-walled basement, and the backyard courtyard beckons with patio tables and string lights.

35 Maryland Ave.
410-626-2020, oldfoxbooks.com

THE BOOKPLATE, CHESTERTOWN

You could easily get lost among the stack-filled rooms at this Chestertown favorite, which specializes in gently worn used books plus select new and regional titles. Everything is tidy and well-marked, so you can easily find what you're seeking, and a cozy performance space hosts author signings and music sessions. Throw in the resident cat, who's always up for a nuzzle, and it feels like home away from home.

112 S. Cross St.
410-778-4167, thebookplate.net

MYSTERY LOVES COMPANY BOOKSTORE, OXFORD

If you love a good sleuth story, head to this shop, set in a hundred-year-old former bank. Owner Kathy Harig stocks mysteries spanning genres from history to science fiction, along with best sellers and a great selection of regional authors. A former librarian, she's a fount of knowledge on books and most anything about the Eastern Shore, and she also curates a slew of author signings.

202 S. Morris St., 800-538-0042, mysterylovescompany.com

BAG THE PERFECT BAG
AT HOBO

I'm always on the lookout for the perfect bag—equal parts chic and useful with the right number of pockets, and well made enough to take a beating—which is why I'm such a fan of HOBO. HOBO-brand bags are sold in shops across the country, but their only standalone store is a three-story townhouse at the foot of Main Street. The bright, loft-style space sells a wide array of backpacks, totes, purses, and wallets. Their smart designs include practical details like easily accessible cell-phone pockets hidden in top seams, plus cool accents from grommets to fringe that reference the boho 1970s without being trendy or overdone. Everything is designed onsite and made from handpicked Italian leather hides, chosen to age beautifully.

194 Green St.
410-349-5081
hobobags.com

TIP
If you're on a budget, head upstairs to the second floor, where they keep their sale items. That's where I typically get into the most trouble.

SCORE SOME SALVAGE
AT IRON WILL WOODWORKS

HGTV fans, put Iron Will Woodworks at the top of your shopping list. Their tagline is "Rebuilding History One Piece at a Time," and that's exactly what happens in this former workshop-turned-store in St. Michaels. Owners Mark and Tracy Miller reclaim antique wood and materials from around the country and repurpose them into heirloom-quality pieces. In this eclectic shop, located in an 1890s flour mill, you'll find everything from tables and cabinets crafted from century-old wood to impeccably restored antique gas pumps, vintage glassware, and a fun selection of local souvenirs such as coasters and candles. Peruse their wood samples and choose your materials for a table or chest made to your specifications. They're expanding into maritime wares as well, with 1950s marina signs and any other treasures they get their hands on.

605 S. Talbot St., St. Michaels
267-221-5107
ironwillwoodworks.com

SUGGESTED
ITINERARIES

FOR THE LOVE OF BOATS

WHEN YOU WANT TO GET NATURAL

HISTORY LOVERS

• •

FOR NON-DIETERS ONLY

ON THE QUIRKY SIDE OF TOWN

THE ARTS HAVE IT

• •

FOR KIDS AND KIDS AT HEART

ITINERARIES
BY SEASON

SPRING

SUMMER

• •

FALL

WINTER

INDEX

• •

• •